QuickBooks Online Practice Set

Gain Experience with Realistic Transactions

Michelle L. Long, CPA, MBA

Andrew S. Long

Copyright © 2013 Michelle L. Long and Andrew S. Long

All rights reserved.

ISBN: 1438298072
ISBN-13: 978-1438298078

DEDICATION

This book is dedicated to all the accountants, bookkeepers and QuickBooks Online users who want more practice using QuickBooks Online. We created this practice set for you to gain more experience and confidence using QuickBooks Online.

MICHELLE L. LONG AND ANDREW S. LONG

ABOUT THE AUTHORS

Michelle L. Long, CPA, MBA is the founder of Long for Success, LLC specializing in QuickBooks Online services and helping small business owners (including accounting professionals) start and grow their business.

Michelle was named one of *10 Women who Inspire a Profession* by Accounting Today, a *Small Business Influencer Awards - Community Choice Winner* by Small Business Trends, and a *Financial Services Champion of the Year* by the Small Business Administration in recognition of her dedication to helping entrepreneurs and small business owners.

As one of the elite national trainers for Intuit, Michelle has presented numerous seminars and webinars and courses for Intuit Academy. She has presented webinars for Staples and Office Depot and spoke at various conferences nationwide. She has been quoted or mentioned in the New York Times, Inc.com, Business Week, Investor's Business Daily, WebCPA, Accounting Today and more.

Michelle is the author of the books *Successful QuickBooks Online Consulting: The Comprehensive Guide to Starting and Growing a QuickBooks Online Consulting Business* and *How to Start a Home-Based Bookkeeping Business* and numerous courses for Intuit Academy.

Since 2000, Michelle has helped tens of thousands of QuickBooks Online users and accounting professionals learn about QuickBooks Online in seminars, webinars and conferences nationwide and recorded QuickBooks Online courses sold on DVD, online video or an iPad app.

Michelle is a CPA, Advanced Certified QuickBooks Online ProAdvisor, holds an MBA in Entrepreneurship and is a Certified FastTrac Facilitator. Her blog was named *10 Accounting Blogs Worth Watching* by Accounting Today. Her Linkedin Group (Successful QuickBooks Online Consultants) has nearly 30,000 members and is a great resource and networking opportunity for accounting professionals.

Andrew S. Long will graduate with a MS in Accountancy from the University of Missouri – Columbia in December 2013. Andrew has made the Dean's List every semester and he has earned numerous scholarships for his academic achievements. Andrew was selected as a member of the prestigious Cornell Leadership Program. He was a member of the Flegel Academy of Aspiring Entrepreneurs and a member of Beta Alpha Psi.

Andrew earned an International Baccalaureate (IB) Diploma and achieved the elite rank of Eagle Scout as well. He likes water and snow skiing and enjoying the outdoors.

Contents

1 INTRODUCTION 3

2 SET UP A NEW COMPANY 5

    Modify the Chart of Accounts 6

    Set up Products and Services 7

    Add New Vendors: 10

    Add New Customers: 10

        Chart of Accounts 11

        Items list 13

        Vendors List 14

        Customers List 14

3 ENTERING TRANSACTIONS – JANUARY 15

    Notes for entering transactions: 15

    January Transactions 16

    Reconcile Accounts 20

    Check Your Progress 21

        Balance Sheet 22

        Profit & Loss 24

        Account Listing 25

        Accounts Payable Aging Detail 27

        Open Purchase Order List 27

Transaction List by Date 28

4 ENTERING TRANSACTIONS – FEBRUARY 29

Notes for entering transactions: 29

February Transactions 30

Reconcile Accounts 38

Check Your Progress 41

Balance Sheet 41

Profit & Loss (Jan 01 - Feb 28) 43

Accounts Receivable Aging Detail 44

Accounts Payable Aging Detail 44

Sales by Customer Detail 45

Sales by Product/Service Detail 48

Inventory Valuation Summary 51

Income List 52

Transaction List by Date 53

5 ENTERING TRANSACTIONS – MARCH 55

Notes for entering transactions: 55

March Transactions 56

Reconcile Accounts 64

Check Your Results 65

Balance Sheet 65

Profit & Loss (Jan 01 - Mar 31) 67

Accounts Receivable Aging Detail 68

Accounts Payable Aging Detail 68

Sales by Customer Detail 69

Sales by Product/Service Detail 73

Inventory Valuation Summary 77

Transaction List by Date 78

ACKNOWLEDGEMENTS

Special thanks to the following individuals for help in reviewing the QuickBooks Practice set which was modified for this QuickBooks Online Practice Set:

Jack E. Cole, Jr.
C*C Systems & Software

Jim Knapp
Knapp Consulting

Janice Boggs
JB's Accounting Solutions

Jo Ellen Peters
Top Notch Bookkeeping

Paula Small
Small Stepping Stones

Trademarks: Intuit, QuickBooks Online, QuickBooks Online Pro, QuickBooks Online Premier, QuickBooks Online Accountant, QuickBooks Online, QuickBooks Online Enterprise, QuickBooks Online Pro for Mac, ProAdvisor, and all other QuickBooks Online references are all trademarks or registered trademarks of Intuit, Inc. Microsoft Windows, Word, Excel are all trademarks or registered trademarks of Microsoft. Macintosh (Mac) is a registered trademark of Apple, Inc. All other brands or products are the trademarks or registered trademarks of their respective holders and should be treated as such.

Author: Please direct your comments or suggestions for future editions to michelle@longforsuccess.com or www.LongforSuccess.com .

1 INTRODUCTION

This practice set is designed to provide realistic transactions for a fictional business (Fitness Haven, LLC) to provide experience using QuickBooks Online. You will set up a new company file, enter three months of transactions, reconcile accounts and check your progress at the end of each month.

This practice set is designed to be used with QuickBooks Online Plus. Go to http://www.QuickBooksOnline.com to register for a free 30 day. Instead of using your regular email address (use it for your regular QuickBooks Online file), use an alternative email for the free trial to use for this practice set.

QuickBooks Online is updated frequently so you may notice some differences in the images. However, you should still be able to enter transactions, reconcile and create reports for this practice set.

This practice set does **not** teach you QuickBooks Online nor accounting or bookkeeping principles. It provides an opportunity for you to get more experience using QuickBooks Online. The ability to check your progress with various reports helps verify that you are entering transactions correctly.

Additionally, this practice set does **not** address nor discuss accounting principles that may vary according to the type of business entity, industry, etc. To simplify this practice set, Fitness Haven, LLC (the fictitious company used in the practice set) does **not** follow GAAP -- i.e. this exercise does not address unearned revenues on membership dues, depreciation on fixed assets, etc. The focus of this practice set is entering transactions common to most small businesses in QuickBooks Online, reconciling and generating reports.

There is a sample company you can use for more practice on your own. You can access it at http://qbo.intuit.com/redir/testdrive

Fitness Haven

In this practice set, business partners Tom Martin, Joe Watson, and Nancy Clemens decide to open a neighborhood fitness center called Fitness Haven. They have been discussing the idea for years and finally decided to take the leap and start the business.

The partners will combine money from their savings and take out a bank loan to finance the gym. They have agreed to forgo a salary or compensation for themselves and to not hire any employees until the business is financially stable (i.e. in the practice set there is no payroll, owner's draws or guaranteed payments).

They will manually write checks and use a credit card for purchases. They plan on buying all the equipment and supplies and leasing (renting) the space for Fitness Haven at a popular neighborhood shopping center. The space they are leasing will need remodeling (leasehold improvements) to get it ready to open. They will purchase exercise equipment and offer classes and personal training sessions in addition to monthly or quarterly memberships.

There will be some retail sales from a few inventory items (bottled water, sports drinks, and nutrition bars). They will purchase a cash register and record weekly sales summaries of these retail sales in QuickBooks Online. All sales are cash or check only (i.e. they do not accept credit cards payments from customers).

You will start by setting up a new company file for Fitness Haven in QuickBooks Online. Next, you will enter transactions during the start-up phase for the first month (January). Then, there are transactions for the next two months (February and March) as well. There are several reports at the end of each month for you to check your work and make corrections if needed.

NOTE: Your QuickBooks Online reports will probably look different from the ones in this practice set. To fit the pertinent information from the report onto the page, we customized many reports (i.e. removed columns, changed the width of columns or made other formatting changes). Focus on the content of the reports (the numbers and details) to check your progress.

If you want to start over or go through the practice set again, you will need to set up another trial subscription to QuickBooks Online (using a different email address).

Note: Please pay attention to the notes throughout the practice set. They contain helpful information.

2 SET UP A NEW COMPANY

On the menu bar, go to Company > Preferences to enter the following information into the appropriate fields. Under the Tax Form section, select the second option (Two or more owners – partnership or LLC). Leave the other fields blank or on their default setting.

Company name (and Legal Name)	Employer ID Number (EIN)	Phone	Address
Fitness Haven, LLC	99-7654321	(654) 555-3476	2601 N Meadow Ln Springfield, IA 68432

Under the Company section, enter the following:
- Tax Form section, select the second option (Two or more owners – partnership or LLC).

Under Products and services:
- Check to enable Products and Services for Sales and for Purchases
- Check to enable Quantity and Price/Rate
- Check to enable Quantity on Hand (Inventory tracking)

Leave the other fields blank or on their default setting.

Click Save (lower, right corner) to save the preferences.

Note: You may need to disable your browser from blocking pop ups as they are frequently used in QuickBooks Online to set up accounts or items.

Modify the Chart of Accounts

1. Open the Chart of Accounts (under the company tab) to add new accounts (Partner's Equity) for Tom, Joe, and Nancy so the equity accounts (with sub-accounts for Partner Contributions and Distributions) are as follows:

   - Tom Martin
     - Tom Partner Contribution
     - Tom Partner Distributions
   - Joe Watson
     - Joe Partner Contribution
     - Joe Partner Distributions
   - Nancy Clemens
     - Nancy Partner Contribution
     - Nancy Partner Distributions

   Note: To set up Tom's accounts, select New (on the bottom right of the chart of accounts page) > Choose from all account types > Next > Equity > Next > Partner's Equity > Next > Partner's Equity > Next > enter "Tom Martin" in the name field. Follow the same process to create the two sub-accounts for except select "Partner Contributions" and "Partner Distributions" on page 4 of 5 and check the box "is sub-account" and select the parent account "Tom Martin" on page 5 of 5 and then hit Finish. Repeat the steps to step up Joe's and Nancy's accounts.

2. Add a Credit Card type account named: Visa

3. Add a Long Term Liability account named: Note Payable – Hometown Bank

4. Add Income accounts (Service/Fee Income type) named Registration Fees and Gym Revenues (for membership fees, classes, and personal training sessions).

Set up Products and Services

First, add a new Sales Tax Item for Springfield, 8% payable to Iowa Department of Revenue. Go to Company > Sales Tax > Set up Sales Tax Rates and make sure both the "Mark all new customers taxable" and the "Mark all new products and services taxable" boxes are checked and then enter the tax information as a single tax rate.

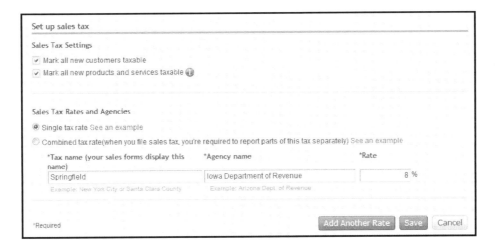

Now go to the Products and Services List (Company > More > Products and Services List) to add Service items for the monthly classes and personal training sessions. Set up the items to post to the Gym Revenues income account. The classes are $50 each and personal training sessions are $35 an hour. Both are non-taxable. **Note**: Do not check to track quantity or purchasing information for these items).

- Personal Training - $35
- Basic Fitness 101 - $50
- Kardio Killers - $50
- Wicked Weights - $50
- Yoga Fitness - $50

Add the following non-taxable service item to post to the Registration Fees income account:

- Registration Fee ($25)

Add the following non-taxable service items to post to the Gym Revenues income account:

- Monthly Membership ($35)
- Quarterly Membership ($90)

Set up Inventory on Products and Services List

Fitness Haven will have a few food items (drinks and nutrition bars) available for sale. A cash register will be used to record the sale of food items (inventory). A weekly summary of sales will be recorded in QuickBooks Online as a Sales Receipt. All sales are paid with cash or checks (no credit cards are accepted from customers).

Note: Important information about setting up inventory on the products and services list:

- Previously you should have checked to enable Quantity on Hand (Inventory Tracking) (Company > Preferences > Products and Services).
- For each product, check the box to Track Quantity on Hand and leave initial quantity on hand as 0 but **change as of date to January 1 of the current year.**
- Flavor varieties should be set up as sub-product/service (i.e. Lemon as a sub-item of Sports Drink) – i.e. check the "is sub-product/service" box and choose the correct parent account.
- All products should be posted to Sales of Product Income and Cost of Goods Sold
- Check the "I purchase this product/service from a vendor" box (on the right side) to input cost information.
- Check the "Is taxable" box under sales information is checked.

Note: Keyboard shortcuts help speed it up – tab through the fields (or use Control+tab to go back through fields) and use the space bar to check a box. Alt+S will save. Creating an Excel file to import them may be more efficient than entering each one individually (but not needed for this practice set).

Item	Unit Cost	Sales Price
Bottled Water	$0.17	$1.50
Sports Drink:		
Lemon	0.37	2.00
Orange	0.37	2.00
Blue	0.37	2.00
Red	0.37	2.00
Energy Drink:		
Regular	1.05	3.75
Sugar-Free	1.05	3.75
Nutrition Bar:		
Chocolate	0.45	3.25
Vanilla	0.45	3.25
Peanut Butter	0.45	3.25

Add New Vendors:

Company	Address	Phone	1099 – ID #
Copper Property Management Co.	423 Eagle Rd Springfield, IA 68432	(654) 555-0122	
Curtis Contractors	8465 Blue Creek Dr Springfield, IA 68432	(654) 555-4876	99-1234567 (Check box to track payments for 1099)
Jones Law Firm	493 Bison Ct Springfield, IA 68432	(654) 555-0937	20-0983456 (Check box to track payments for 1099)
Life Fitness Co.	12576 Trailview Rd Springfield, IA 68432	(654) 555-4069	

Add New Customers:

Customer	Address	Phone
Adrian Gonzalez	324 Birdsong Way Springfield, IA 68432	(654) 555-5632
Daniel Brown	782 Locust Ave Springfield, IA 68432	(654) 555-5890
Lucy Hopper	8326 Waterfall Ln Springfield, IA 68432	(654) 555-6264

Throughout the Practice Set, as you enter transactions for new customers or vendors, use the Quick Add feature to add them. **Note**: this practice set contains address information only. In a real business situation, you may need to include more details such as emails, terms, custom fields or more.

QUICKBOOKS ONLINE PRACTICE SET

Check your Progress

Chart of Accounts

Here is what the Chart of Accounts looks like (Reports > Account Listing). You can access this report by clicking on Reports > Report List > Account Listing.

Note: For this and all other reports shown throughout the practice set, the reports were modified to show only the most relevant information due to space restrictions so your reports may look different. For example, in this report all columns were removed except the 3 most important columns as shown here.

Account	Type	Detail type
Inventory Asset	Other Current Assets	Inventory
Prepaid Expenses	Other Current Assets	Prepaid Expenses
Undeposited Funds	Other Current Assets	Undeposited Funds
Visa	Credit Card	Credit Card
Note Payable - Hometown Bank	Long Term Liabilities	Notes Payable
Joe Watson	Equity	Partner's Equity
Joe Watson:Partner Contributions	Equity	Partner Contributions
Joe Watson:Partner Distributions	Equity	Partner Distributions
Nancy Clemens	Equity	Partner's Equity
Nancy Clemens:Partner Contributions	Equity	Partner Contributions
Nancy Clemens:Partner Distributions	Equity	Partner Distributions
Retained Earnings	Equity	Retained Earnings
Tom Martin	Equity	Partner's Equity
Tom Martin:Partner Contributions	Equity	Partner Contributions
Tom Martin:Partner Distributions	Equity	Partner Distributions
Discounts	Income	Discounts/Refunds Given
Gross Receipts	Income	Sales of Product Income
Gym Revenues	Income	Service/Fee Income
Refunds-Allowances	Income	Discounts/Refunds Given
Registration Fees	Income	Service/Fee Income
Sales	Income	Sales of Product Income
Sales of Product Income	Income	Sales of Product Income
Shipping, Delivery Income	Income	Other Primary Income
Cost of Goods Sold	Cost of Goods Sold	Supplies & Materials - COGS
Cost of labor - COS	Cost of Goods Sold	Cost of labor - COS
Freight & delivery - COS	Cost of Goods Sold	Shipping, Freight & Delivery - COS
Other Costs - COS	Cost of Goods Sold	Other Costs of Services - COS
Purchases - COS	Cost of Goods Sold	Other Costs of Services - COS
Subcontractors - COS	Cost of Goods Sold	Cost of labor - COS
Supplies & Materials - COGS	Cost of Goods Sold	Supplies & Materials - COGS
Advertising	Expenses	Advertising/Promotional
Bad Debts	Expenses	Bad Debts
Bank Charges	Expenses	Bank Charges
Commissions & fees	Expenses	Other Miscellaneous Service Cost

Disposal Fees	Expenses	Other Miscellaneous Service Cost
Dues & Subscriptions	Expenses	Dues & subscriptions
Freight & Delivery	Expenses	Shipping, Freight & Delivery
Insurance	Expenses	Insurance
Insurance - Disability	Expenses	Insurance
Insurance - Liability	Expenses	Insurance
Interest Expense	Expenses	Interest Paid
Job Materials	Expenses	Supplies & Materials
Legal & Professional Fees	Expenses	Legal & Professional Fees
Meals and Entertainment	Expenses	Entertainment Meals
Office Expenses	Expenses	Office/General Administrative Expenses
Other General and Admin Expenses	Expenses	Office/General Administrative Expenses
Promotional	Expenses	Advertising/Promotional
Purchases	Expenses	Supplies & Materials
Rent or Lease	Expenses	Rent or Lease of Buildings
Repair & Maintenance	Expenses	Repair & Maintenance
Shipping and delivery expense	Expenses	Shipping, Freight & Delivery
Stationery & Printing	Expenses	Office/General Administrative Expenses
Subcontractors	Expenses	Cost of Labor
Supplies	Expenses	Supplies & Materials
Taxes & Licenses	Expenses	Taxes Paid
Tools	Expenses	Supplies & Materials
Travel	Expenses	Travel
Travel Meals	Expenses	Travel Meals
Utilities	Expenses	Utilities
Interest Earned	Other Income	Interest Earned
Other Ordinary Income	Other Income	Other Miscellaneous Income
Other Portfolio Income	Other Income	Other Miscellaneous Income
Miscellaneous	Other Expense	Other Miscellaneous Expense
Penalties & Settlements	Other Expense	Penalties & Settlements

QUICKBOOKS ONLINE PRACTICE SET

Items list

You can access this report by clicking on Reports > Report List > Product/Service List (Under the Lists category, near the bottom).

Can't run

Again – only relevant columns are shown here.

Product/Service	Price	Cost
Basic Fitness 101	50.00	
Bottled Water	1.50	0.17
Energy Drink		
Energy Drink:Regular	3.75	1.05
Energy Drink:Sugar-Free	3.75	1.05
Hours		
Kardio Killers	50.00	
Monthly Membership	35.00	
Nutrition Bar		
Nutrition Bar:Chocolate	3.25	0.45
Nutrition Bar:Peanut Butter	3.25	0.45
Nutrition Bar:Vanilla	3.25	0.45
Personal Training	35.00	
Quarterly Membership	90.00	
Registration Fee	25.00	
Sales		
Sports Drink		
Sports Drink:Blue	2.00	0.37
Sports Drink:Lemon	2.00	0.37
Sports Drink:Orange	2.00	0.37
Sports Drink:Red	2.00	0.37
Wicked Weights	50.00	
Yoga Fitness	50.00	

Vendors List

You can view the vendors list by clicking on Reports > Report List > Vendor Contact List.

Vendor	Phone Numbers	Full Name	Address
Copper Property Management Co.	Phone: (654) 555-0122	Copper Property Management Co.	423 Eagle Rd Springfield IA 68432
Curtis Contractors	Phone: (654) 555-4876	Curtis Contractors	8465 Blue Creek Dr. Springfield IA 68432
Jones Law Firm	Phone: (654) 555-0937	Jones Law Firm	493 Bison Ct Springfield IA 68432
Life Fitness Co.	Phone: (654) 555-4069	Life Fitness Co.	12576 Trailview Rd Springfield IA 68432

Customers List

You can view the customers list by clicking on Reports > Report List > Customer Contact List.

Client	Phone Numbers	Full Name	Billing Address
Adrian Gonzalez	Phone: (654) 555-5632	Adrian Gonzalez	324 Birdsong Way Springfield IA 68432
Daniel Brown	Phone: (654) 555-5890	Daniel Brown	728 Locust Ave Springfield IA 68432
Lucy Hopper	Phone: (654) 555-6264	Lucy Hopper	8326 Waterfall Ln Springfield IA 68432

3 ENTERING TRANSACTIONS – JANUARY

Enter the following transactions for January. For this practice set, post the following transactions to the appropriate account based on the expenditure (i.e. do not post anything to start-up expenses). In a real situation, you should consult with an accountant or tax professional for guidance on accounting for start-up costs.

Notes for entering transactions:

- Use Accounts Payable for monthly expenses and bills. When transactions say "Received a Bill" (Enter a Bill) and Pay Bills when indicated.

- Enter Checks or Credit Card Charges as indicated for purchases from local retailers and others.

- Quick Add Customers and Vendors as needed (the partners should be set up as a vendor).

- Create new accounts as needed and do not worry about depreciation on fixed asset accounts.

Navigating Tips

Google Chrome is the recommended browser for QuickBooks Online and you can download it free (like Firefox or Internet Explorer). In all browsers, you can have multiple tabs or windows open (tabbed browsing). In Chrome, you can right click on the tab and select Duplicate. In other browsers, Control+N (Cmd+N on a Mac) will open another window / browser tab. Plus, you can drag & drop to re-arrange the open tabs or move a window to another monitor. This allows you to have multiple windows open when working in QuickBooks Online which can help improve efficiency. Use Google or Help for your browser to learn more about tabbed browsing.

Additionally, with Google Chrome you can create multiple user accounts. This allows you to login to multiple QuickBooks Online companies simultaneously. However, pay careful attention to the user icon to monitor which company you are currently using. It is easy to make changes to the wrong company file. This article explains how to set up and use multiple users in Google Chrome: https://support.google.com/chrome/answer/2364824?hl=en

January Transactions

1. Jan 4: The partners (Tom Martin, Joe Watson, and Nancy Clemens) contribute $5,000.00 each to open the Fitness Haven checking account at Hometown Bank with an initial deposit totaling $15,000.00.

   Note: Add a bank account (checking) for Hometown Bank (no opening balance). Enter a deposit for the $15,000 posting it to the Owner's Contribution accounts for each partner (Click on Banking > Deposits). Click no on the 2 interview questions when it pops up. Quick Add each partner as a Vendor so details of their activity will be shown in the Vendor Center.

   TIP: It saves time to set up Online Banking in QuickBooks Online and download transactions. You can practice with downloaded transactions in the sample company here: http://qbo.intuit.com/redir/testdrive -- go to Banking, Downloaded Transactions (or Online Banking).

   TIP: You can use the + or – key to move the date forward or backward quickly as you enter transactions. Also, if you enter T in the date field, it will use Today's date.

2. Jan 7: Deposited loan proceeds of $250,000.00 for the Note Payable from Hometown Bank into checking account.

3. Jan 8: Check #1001 to Copper Property Management Co. in the amount of $4,500.00 ($3,000.00 for security deposit and $1,500.00 for January rent).

   Note: Type Security Deposit and it will prompt you to add the new account, select Choose from all account types > Other Assets > Security Deposits.

4. Jan 9: Check #1002 to Jones Law Firm in the amount of $1,785.00 for legal fees for the partnership agreement.

5. Jan 17: Check #1003 to Curtis Contractors in the amount of $52,736.89 for Leasehold Improvements.

   Note: Create a new fixed asset account for the Leasehold Improvements and select no when it asks if you want to track depreciation. In the last step, do not enter an existing balance.

6. Jan 18: Check #1004 to Life Fitness Co. in the amount of $80,000.00 for the purchase of exercise equipment.

Fixed Asset Item	Total Price
Treadmills (5)	$10,000
Stationary Bikes (5)	12,000
Elliptical Machines (5)	10,000
Weight Machines (10)	40,000
Free Weights (2 sets)	8,000

Note: QuickBooks Online does not have a fixed asset items list so instead set up a new account called Fitness Equipment as a Machinery & Equipment fixed asset account (choose to not track depreciation and do not enter a cost). Add fixed asset accounts for each of the 5 different kinds of equipment purchased as sub-accounts of the Fitness Equipment account. Put the quantity in the description field of the itemize by account section when writing the check (not when setting up the account).

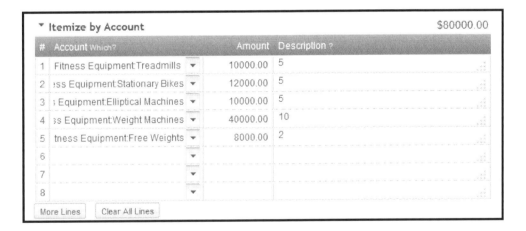

7. Jan 21: Charged $136.67 on Visa credit card at Wal-Mart for office expenses.

8. Jan 21: Check #1005 to Costco in the amount of $2,400 for the following office equipment:

   Note: Set up a new account called Office Furniture and Equipment as a Machinery & Equipment fixed asset account (choose to not track depreciation and do not enter a cost). This time you do not need to create a separate account for each item, just note in the description the items purchased.

Fixed Asset Item	Total Price
Cash Register	$1,200
Computer	1,000
Printer	200

9. Jan 22: Purchase order #1001 to Fit Foods, Inc. in the amount of $126.48 to purchase the following inventory items:

Item	Quantity	Unit Cost	Total Cost	Sales Price
Bottled Water	48	$0.17	$8.16	$1.50
Sports Drink:				
Lemon	24	0.37	8.88	2.00
Orange	24	0.37	8.88	2.00
Blue	24	0.37	8.88	2.00
Red	24	0.37	8.88	2.00
Energy Drink:				
Regular	24	1.05	25.20	3.75
Sugar-Free	24	1.05	25.20	3.75
Nutrition Bar:				
Chocolate	24	0.45	10.80	3.25
Vanilla	24	0.45	10.80	3.25
Peanut Butter	24	0.45	10.80	3.25

10. Jan 23: Check #1006 to Geek Squad in the amount of $250.00 to set up and configure computers and network (set up a Computer and Internet Expense account under the Office/General and Administrative category).

11. Jan 25: Check #1007 to Super Signs in the amount of $1,200.00 for purchase of outdoor signage (set up a fixed asset, furniture and fixtures account).

12. Jan 26: Check #1008 to ABC Web Designs in the amount of $300.00 for website creation (a computer and internet expense).

13. Jan 28: Check #1009 to Val-Pak in the amount of $225.00 for advertising in their direct mail packet.

14. Jan 29: Charged $1,723.15 on Visa credit card at Office Depot for the following office furniture:

Fixed Asset Item	Total Price
Desk (2)	$1,567.39
Chairs (2)	155.76

Note: Post it to the Office Furniture and Equipment account and note the items in the description.

15. Jan 31: Received bill from Time Warner in the amount of $147.62 for phone and internet service with terms of net 30 (n/30).

    Note: Make Phone/Internet a sub-account of utilities expense. Also create a sub-account for the each of the following three bills (electricity, water, trash removal).

16. Jan 31: Received bill from Metro Electric Co. in the amount of $183.86 for electricity with terms of n/30.

17. Jan 31: Received bill from City of Springfield in the amount of for $51.45 for water with terms of n/30.

18. Jan 31: Received bill from Waste Management in the amount of $45.00 for trash removal with terms of n/30.

Reconcile Accounts

Use the following information to reconcile the checking account (Banking > More > Reconcile):

Bank Statement Ending Date	1/31/2013
Bank Statement Ending Balance	$122,128.11
Outstanding Checks: Check #1008 -- $300 Check #1009 -- $225	

```
Total Cleared Transactions                                              122,128.11
Uncleared Transactions as of 01/31/2013

Date              Type          Num       Payee                          Amount
Uncleared Checks and Payments
01/26/2013        Check         1008      ABC Web Designs                 300.00
01/28/2013        Check         1009      Val-Pak                         225.00
                                                                  Subtotal: 525.00
Uncleared Deposits and Other Credits
                                                                    Subtotal: 0.00

Total Uncleared Transactions as of 01/31/2013                            -525.00

Subtotal: 01/31/2013                                                       0.00
```

Use the following information to reconcile the Visa credit card account:

Bank Statement Ending Date	1/31/2013
Bank Statement Ending Balance	$1,859.82
Outstanding Items: None	

After reconciling the credit card account, select to write a check for payment now. Enter the payment date of Feb. 1, payable to Great American Bank (Quick Add as a vendor). The check number is 1010.

Check Your Progress

Create the following reports and compare them to the results shown (focus on totals – it is ok if accounts are in a different order than what is shown here). Make sure you change the report date for this and all other reports so that it displays the proper period (in this case as of 1/31/13). Throughout this practice set, you may notice the reports shown look different than the reports you generate (some columns missing, different column widths, etc.). This is due space constraints which require customizing the reports to fit in this practice set. These differences are cosmetic only; the numbers shown should match your own.

Note: Select accrual basis for reports when a pop up appears after you run the first report.

TIP: In QuickBooks Online, you can schedule memorized reports to be emailed automatically. Under memorized reports, select the report and edit to set the email schedule for the report. You can also create a group of memorized reports and schedule the group to be emailed.

MICHELLE L. LONG AND ANDREW S. LONG

Balance Sheet

Note: This report can be found by clicking on Reports > Report List > Balance Sheet (under the company section).

As of January 31, 2013

	Total
ASSETS	
Current Assets	
Bank Accounts	
Hometown Bank	121,603.11
Total Bank Accounts	**121,603.11**
Total Current Assets	**121,603.11**
Fixed Assets	
Fitness Equipment	
Elliptical Machines	10,000.00
Free Weights	8,000.00
Stationary Bikes	12,000.00
Treadmills	10,000.00
Weight Machines	40,000.00
Total Fitness Equipment	**80,000.00**
Furniture and Equipment	1,200.00
Leasehold Improvements	52,736.89
Office Furniture and Equipment	4,123.15
Total Fixed Assets	**138,060.04**
Other Assets	
Security Deposit	3,000.00
Total Other Assets	**3,000.00**
TOTAL ASSETS	**262,663.15**
LIABILITIES AND EQUITY	
Liabilities	
Current Liabilities	
Accounts Payable	
Accounts Payable (A/P)	427.93
Total Accounts Payable	**427.93**
Credit Cards	
Visa	1,859.82
Total Credit Cards	**1,859.82**
Total Current Liabilities	**2,287.75**
Long-Term Liabilities	

Note Payable - Hometown Bank	250,000.00
Total Long-Term Liabilities	**250,000.00**
Total Liabilities	**252,287.75**
Equity	
Joe Watson	
Partner Contributions	5,000.00
Total Joe Watson	**5,000.00**
Nancy Clemens	
Partner Contributions	5,000.00
Total Nancy Clemens	**5,000.00**
Retained Earnings	
Tom Martin	
Partner Contributions	5,000.00
Total Tom Martin	**5,000.00**
Net Income	(4,624.60)
Total Equity	**10,375.40**
TOTAL LIABILITIES AND EQUITY	**262,663.15**

Profit & Loss

Note: This report can be found under the company section of the report list.

January 2013

	Total
Income	
Total Income	
Gross Profit	-
Expenses	
Advertising	225.00
Computer and Internet Expense	550.00
Legal & Professional Fees	1,785.00
Rent or Lease	1,500.00
Supplies	136.67
Utilities	
Electricity	183.86
Phone/Internet	147.62
Trash Removal	45.00
Water	51.45
Total Utilities	**427.93**
Total Expenses	**4,624.60**
Net Operating Income	**(4,624.60)**
Net Income	**(4,624.60)**

QUICKBOOKS ONLINE PRACTICE SET

Account Listing

Note: This report can be found under the lists section of the report list.

Account	Type	Detail type	Balance
Hometown Bank	Bank	Checking	119,743.29
Inventory Asset	Other Current Assets	Inventory	0.00
Prepaid Expenses	Other Current Assets	Prepaid Expenses	0.00
Uncategorized Asset	Other Current Assets	Other Current Assets	0.00
Undeposited Funds	Other Current Assets	Undeposited Funds	0.00
Fitness Equipment	Fixed Assets	Machinery & Equipment	80,000.00
Fitness Equipment:Elliptical Machines	Fixed Assets	Machinery & Equipment	10,000.00
Fitness Equipment:Free Weights	Fixed Assets	Machinery & Equipment	8,000.00
Fitness Equipment:Stationary Bikes	Fixed Assets	Machinery & Equipment	12,000.00
Fitness Equipment:Treadmills	Fixed Assets	Machinery & Equipment	10,000.00
Fitness Equipment:Weight Machines	Fixed Assets	Machinery & Equipment	40,000.00
Furniture and Equipment	Fixed Assets	Furniture & Fixtures	1,200.00
Leasehold Improvements	Fixed Assets	Leasehold Improvements	52,736.89
Office Furniture and Equipment	Fixed Assets	Machinery & Equipment	4,123.15
Security Deposit	Other Assets	Security Deposits	3,000.00
Accounts Payable (A/P)	Accounts payable (A/P)	Accounts Payable (A/P)	-427.93
Visa	Credit Card	Credit Card	0.00
Note Payable - Hometown Bank	Long Term Liabilities	Notes Payable	-250,000.00
Joe Watson	Equity	Partner's Equity	-5,000.00
Joe Watson:Partner Contributions	Equity	Partner Contributions	-5,000.00
Joe Watson:Partner Distributions	Equity	Partner Distributions	0.00
Nancy Clemens	Equity	Partner's Equity	-5,000.00
Nancy Clemens:Partner Contributions	Equity	Partner Contributions	-5,000.00
Nancy Clemens:Partner Distributions	Equity	Partner Distributions	0.00
Retained Earnings	Equity	Retained Earnings	0.00
Tom Martin	Equity	Partner's Equity	-5,000.00
Tom Martin:Partner Contributions	Equity	Partner Contributions	-5,000.00
Tom Martin:Partner Distributions	Equity	Partner Distributions	0.00
Discounts	Income	Discounts/Refunds Given	
Gross Receipts	Income	Sales of Product Income	
Gym Revenues	Income	Service/Fee Income	
Refunds-Allowances	Income	Discounts/Refunds Given	
Registration Fees	Income	Service/Fee Income	
Sales	Income	Sales of Product Income	
Sales of Product Income	Income	Sales of Product Income	
Shipping, Delivery Income	Income	Other Primary Income	
Uncategorized Income	Income	Sales of Product Income	
Cost of Goods Sold	Cost of Goods Sold	Supplies & Materials - COGS	
Cost of labor - COS	Cost of Goods Sold	Cost of labor - COS	
Freight & delivery - COS	Cost of Goods Sold	Shipping, Freight & Delivery - COS	
Other Costs - COS	Cost of Goods Sold	Other Costs of Services - COS	
Purchases - COS	Cost of Goods Sold	Other Costs of Services - COS	
Subcontractors - COS	Cost of Goods Sold	Cost of labor - COS	
Supplies & Materials - COGS	Cost of Goods Sold	Supplies & Materials -	

		COGS
Advertising	Expenses	Advertising/Promotional
Bad Debts	Expenses	Bad Debts
Bank Charges	Expenses	Bank Charges
Commissions & fees	Expenses	Other Miscellaneous Service Cost
Computer and Internet Expense	Expenses	Office/General Administrative Expenses
Disposal Fees	Expenses	Other Miscellaneous Service Cost
Dues & Subscriptions	Expenses	Dues & subscriptions
Freight & Delivery	Expenses	Shipping, Freight & Delivery
Insurance	Expenses	Insurance
Insurance - Disability	Expenses	Insurance
Insurance - Liability	Expenses	Insurance
Interest Expense	Expenses	Interest Paid
Job Materials	Expenses	Supplies & Materials
Legal & Professional Fees	Expenses	Legal & Professional Fees
Meals and Entertainment	Expenses	Entertainment Meals
Office Expenses	Expenses	Office/General Administrative Expenses
Other General and Admin Expenses	Expenses	Office/General Administrative Expenses
Promotional	Expenses	Advertising/Promotional
Purchases	Expenses	Supplies & Materials
Rent or Lease	Expenses	Rent or Lease of Buildings
Repair & Maintenance	Expenses	Repair & Maintenance
Shipping and delivery expense	Expenses	Shipping, Freight & Delivery
Stationery & Printing	Expenses	Office/General Administrative Expenses
Subcontractors	Expenses	Cost of Labor
Supplies	Expenses	Supplies & Materials
Taxes & Licenses	Expenses	Taxes Paid
Tools	Expenses	Supplies & Materials
Travel	Expenses	Travel
Travel Meals	Expenses	Travel Meals
Uncategorized Expense	Expenses	Other Miscellaneous Service Cost
Utilities	Expenses	Utilities
Utilities:Electricity	Expenses	Utilities
Utilities:Phone/Internet	Expenses	Utilities
Utilities:Trash Removal	Expenses	Utilities
Utilities:Water	Expenses	Utilities
Interest Earned	Other Income	Interest Earned
Other Ordinary Income	Other Income	Other Miscellaneous Income
Other Portfolio Income	Other Income	Other Miscellaneous Income
Miscellaneous	Other Expense	Other Miscellaneous Expense
Penalties & Settlements	Other Expense	Penalties & Settlements

Accounts Payable Aging Detail

Note: This report can be found under the vendors section of the report list. QuickBooks Online may tell you these are past due depending on what date you entered.

As of January 31, 2013

	Date	Transaction Type	Vendor	Due Date	Amount	Open Balance
Current						
	01/31/2013	Bill	Waste Management	03/02/2013	45.00	45.00
	01/31/2013	Bill	Time Warner	03/02/2013	147.62	147.62
	01/31/2013	Bill	Metro Electric Co.	03/02/2013	183.86	183.86
	01/31/2013	Bill	City of Springfield	03/02/2013	51.45	51.45
Total for Current					427.93	427.93
TOTAL					427.93	427.93

Open Purchase Order List

Note: This report can be found under the vendor section of the report list.

	Date	Num	Memo/Description	Ship Via	Amount
Fit Foods, Inc.					
	01/22/2013	1001			126.48

Transaction List by Date

Note: This report can be found under the accountant & taxes section of the report list.

Date	Transaction Type	Num	Posting	Name	Account	Split	Amount
01/04/2013	Deposit		Yes		Hometown Bank	-Split-	15,000.00
01/07/2013	Deposit		Yes		Hometown Bank	Note Payable - Hometown Bank	250,000.00
01/08/2013	Check	1001	Yes	Copper Property Management Co.	Hometown Bank	-Split-	-4,500.00
01/09/2013	Check	1002	Yes	Jones Law Firm	Hometown Bank	Legal & Professional Fees	-1,785.00
01/17/2013	Check	1003	Yes	Curtis Contractors	Hometown Bank	Leasehold Improvements	-52,736.89
01/18/2013	Check	1004	Yes	Life Fitness Co.	Hometown Bank	-Split-	-80,000.00
01/21/2013	Credit Card Expense		Yes	Wal-Mart	Visa	Supplies	136.67
01/21/2013	Check	1005	Yes	Costco	Hometown Bank	Office Furniture and Equipment	-2,400.00
01/22/2013	Purchase Order	1001	No	Fit Foods, Inc.	Accounts Payable (A/P)	-Split-	126.48
01/23/2013	Check	1006	Yes	Geek Squad	Hometown Bank	Computer and Internet Expense	-250.00
01/25/2013	Check	1007	Yes	Super Signs	Hometown Bank	Furniture and Equipment	-1,200.00
01/26/2013	Check	1008	Yes	ABC Web Designs	Hometown Bank	Computer and Internet Expense	-300.00
01/28/2013	Check	1009	Yes	Val-Pak	Hometown Bank	Advertising	-225.00
01/29/2013	Credit Card Expense		Yes	Office Depot	Visa	Office Furniture and Equipment	1,723.15
01/31/2013	Bill		Yes	Time Warner	Accounts Payable (A/P)	Utilities:Phone/Internet	147.62
01/31/2013	Bill		Yes	Metro Electric Co.	Accounts Payable (A/P)	Utilities:Electricity	183.86
01/31/2013	Bill		Yes	City of Springfield	Accounts Payable (A/P)	Utilities:Water	51.45
01/31/2013	Bill		Yes	Waste Management	Accounts Payable (A/P)	Utilities:Trash Removal	45.00

4 ENTERING TRANSACTIONS – FEBRUARY

Fitness Haven opens on February 4th and offers two membership options.

- **Monthly**: New members pay a one-time registration fee of $25 and $35 month membership fees.
- **Quarterly**: Members pay three months of membership dues in advance (only $30 / month). The 3 month membership is non-refundable.

Notes for entering transactions:

- Use a Sales Receipt for initial registration fees and membership dues received. Subsequent membership dues will be entered as an Invoice and then Receive Payment.

- Enter Sales Receipts for classes and personal training sessions.

- Payments received should go to Undeposited Funds. Leave them in Undeposited Funds until the transaction (weekly) to Record Deposits.

- Use Accounts Payable (i.e. Enter Bills and Pay Bills) for monthly expenses and bills (when transactions say Received Bill and Pay Bills).

- Enter Checks as indicated for purchases from local retailers and others.

- Do not worry about depreciation on fixed assets. It is assumed the accountant or tax professional maintains details of fixed assets and depreciation.

February Transactions

1. Feb 1: Check #1011 to Oak Hill Homeowners Association in the amount of $150.00 for an ad in their newsletter.

2. Feb 3: Check #1012 to Willy's Windows in the amount of $75.00 for window cleaning (repairs and maintenance).

3. Feb 3: Received inventory and the bill ($126.48) from Fit Foods, Inc. for all items ordered on Purchase Order #1, the terms are n/30. (Go to Enter Bill from Fit Foods and click Add Purchase Order).

4. Feb 4: Lucy Steele paid $25 for a first time gym registration fee and a monthly membership fee of $35 (total received $60). (Enter a Sales Receipt)

    Note: Be sure to check "Group with other Undeposited Funds" under the payment information section since Fitness Haven only makes weekly deposits.

5. Feb 4: Jerry Kline paid $25 for a first time gym registration fee and a monthly membership fee of $35 (total received $60). (Sales Receipt)

6. Feb 4: Received bill from Yoga Bliss, LLC in the amount of $235.00 for yoga mats and towels (i.e. fitness supplies – create a new expense account – detail type Supplies & Materials) with terms of 2% 10, Net 30 (add new term 2/10, n/30 – 2% discount if paid within 10 days, net due in 30 days).

7. Feb 4: Jim Hill paid $25 for a first time gym registration fee and a monthly membership fee of $35. (Sales Receipt)

8. Feb 4: Augusto Gutierrez paid $90 for a Quarterly Membership (i.e. 3 months of gym membership). For Quarterly memberships, the monthly rate is discounted to $30/month and the registration fee is waived because of prepayment. (Sales Receipt)

9. Feb 5: Check #1013 to Long for Success, LLC in the amount of $450.00 for QuickBooks Online setup and training (Create a new account for accounting fees as a sub-account of Legal & Professional Fees).

10. Feb 6: Sent invoices to Adrian Gonzalez, Daniel Brown, and Lucy Hopper in the amount of $35 each for February gym membership (Monthly membership) with terms of n/10 (add new terms). Their gym registration fee was waived because they signed up in advance.

    TIP: You could send (email) the invoices to customers or make the invoice recurring (since it is a monthly membership). However, we won't do either in this practice set.

11. Feb 7: The following table lists the members who signed up and paid for February fitness classes (i.e. enter a Sales Receipt for each one). All classes are $50.

Basic Fitness 101	Wicked Weights	Kardio Killers	Yoga Fitness
Jerry Kline	Daniel Brown		
Adrian Gonzalez	Jim Hill		
Lucy Steele			

12. Feb 7: Tim Barnes paid $25 for a first time gym registration fee and a monthly membership fee of $35. (Sales Receipt)

13. Feb 7: Sold 1 hour of personal training to Tim Barnes for $35. (Sales Receipt)

14. Feb 7: Received payment of $35 from Adrian Gonzalez for February gym membership.

    Note: For all received payment transactions, select check as the payment method and select "Group with other Undeposited funds."

15. Feb 7: Total food sales from the week are shown in the table below:

    Note: Add a customer named Weekly Sales and enter a Sales Receipt for the weekly sales, selecting the 8% tax rate in the tax field.

Item	Quantity Sold	Sales Price	Totals
Bottled Water		$1.50	
Sports Drink:			
Lemon		2.00	
Orange	2	2.00	$4.00
Blue	2	2.00	4.00
Red		2.00	
Energy Drink:			
Regular		3.75	
Sugar-Free		3.75	
Nutrition Bar:			

Chocolate	1	3.25	3.25
Vanilla		3.25	
Peanut Butter		3.25	
Subtotal			11.25
Sales Tax			0.90
Total			12.15

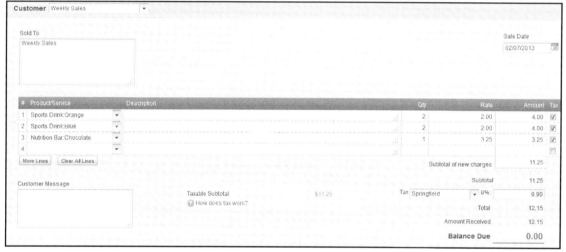

16. Feb 7: Deposited all Undeposited funds from the first week of the month into the checking account by going to Banking > Deposits and click select all (total deposit $662.15).

17. Feb 8: Recorded inventory adjustment: loss of 6 sugar-free energy drinks. A 6-pack of drinks was dropped and all cans were punctured.

    Note: Go to the Products and Services List and double-click on sugar-free energy drink and click "Update." Enter Difference of -6 and the new quantity on hand will calculate automatically. An adjustment will be posted to inventory and inventory shrinkage as of Feb 8.

18. Feb 8: Check #1014 to Copper Property Management Co. in the amount of $1,500.00 for February rent.

19. Feb 10: Robert Markum paid $25 for a first time gym registration fee and a monthly membership fee of $35.

20. Feb 10: Sold 1 hour of personal training to Adrian Gonzalez for $35 (Sales Receipt).

21. Feb 11: Received payment of $35 from Lucy Hopper for February gym membership (previously invoiced).

22. Feb 12: Charged $68.97 on Visa credit card at Wal-Mart for cleaning supplies (set up a new account).

23. Feb 14: Julie Stein paid $90 for a quarterly (3 months) gym membership.

24. Feb 14: Total food sales from the week are shown in the table below:

Item	Quantity Sold	Sales Price	Totals
Bottled Water		$1.50	
Sports Drink:			
Lemon	3	2.00	$6.00
Orange		2.00	
Blue	2	2.00	4.00
Red	1	2.00	2.00
Energy Drink:			
Regular		3.75	
Sugar-Free	2	3.75	7.50
Nutrition Bar:			
Chocolate	3	3.25	9.75
Vanilla		3.25	
Peanut Butter		3.25	
Subtotal			**29.25**
Sales Tax			**2.34**
Total			**31.59**

25. Feb 14: Deposited all Undeposited funds from the second week of the month into the checking account. (Total Deposit $251.59)

26. Feb 14: Received payment of $35 from Daniel Brown for February gym membership (previously invoiced).

27. Feb 15: Paid bill from Yoga Bliss, LLC with Hand Written Check #1015 in the amount of $235 (Go to Vendors > Pay Bills and select the one from Yoga Bliss and be sure to enter the correct payment date).

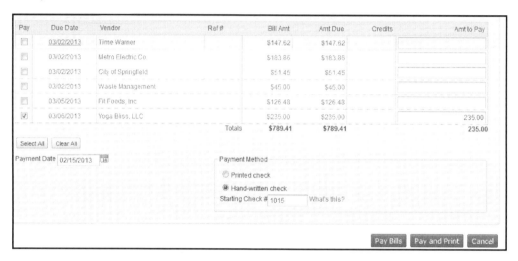

28. Feb 15: Issued a partial refund to Jim Hill for $20 because he sustained an injury and cannot use the rest of his month's membership.

Note: Go to Customer > More > Refund or Credit. This may trigger multiple pop up interviews in which case just leave the settings and default choices as they are and click next through them until you return to the refund page. Enter the customer name and enter the credit for the Item of Monthly Membership and change the amount to $20. Select Check as the payment method (#1016) in the Refund Information section and click Save.

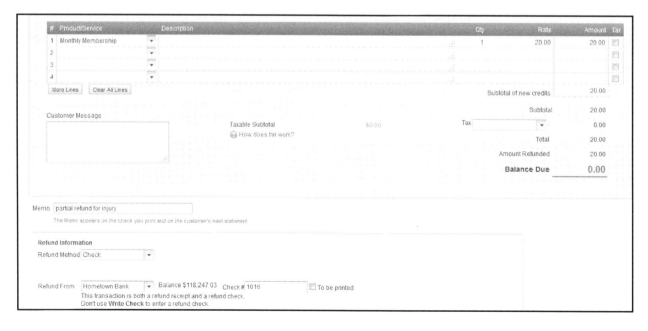

29. Feb 16: Cindy Blackburn paid $25 for a first time gym registration fee and a monthly membership fee of $35.

30. Feb 18: Received bill from Swisher Marketing, LLC in the amount of $750.00 for direct mail marketing campaign with terms of n/30. (Advertising expense)

31. Feb 20: Christopher Tomlinson paid $25 for a first time gym registration fee and a monthly membership fee of $35.

32. Feb 21: Total food sales from the week are shown in the table below:

Item	Quantity Sold	Sales Price	Totals
Bottled Water	3	$1.50	$4.50
Sports Drink:			
Lemon		2.00	
Orange	1	2.00	2.00
Blue	4	2.00	8.00
Red		2.00	
Energy Drink:			
Regular		3.75	
Sugar-Free	3	3.75	11.25
Nutrition Bar:			
Chocolate	1	3.25	3.25
Vanilla	2	3.25	6.50
Peanut Butter	1	3.25	3.25
Subtotal			**38.75**
Sales Tax			**3.10**
Total			**41.85**

33. Feb 21: Deposited all Undeposited funds from the third week of the month into the checking account. Total Deposit is $196.85.

34. Feb 22: Sent invoices to the following members in the amount of $35 for March membership (i.e. Monthly membership) with terms of n/30:

- Daniel Brown
- Adrian Gonzalez
- Lucy Steele
- Jerry Kline
- Tim Barnes
- Robert Markum
- Cindy Blackburn

Note: Lucy Hopper, Jim Hill, and Christopher Tomlinson decided to not renew their membership.

TIP: After you create one invoice, you can click Copy and change the name for the next customer. This saves time when entering multiple invoices.

35. Feb 23: Lynn Sampson paid $90 for a quarterly gym membership.

36. Feb 25: Paid bill from Swisher Marketing, LLC. in the amount of $750.00 with check #1017.

37. Feb 26: Sold 2 hours of personal training to Adrian Gonzalez for a total of $70.

38. Feb 28: Charged $56.70 on Visa credit card at Office Depot for printer ink (office expenses).

39. Feb 28: Paid all outstanding bills. Total paid $554.41 and let QuickBooks Online assign check numbers 1018 through 1022.

40. Feb 28: Received bill from Time Warner in the amount of $147.62 for phone, internet, and cable services with terms of n/30.

41. Feb 28: Received bill from Metro Electric Co. in the amount of $178.86 for electricity with terms of n/30.

42. Feb 28: Received bill from City of Springfield in the amount of for $86.45 for water with terms of n/30.

43. Feb 28: Received bill from Waste Management in the amount of $45.00 for trash removal with terms of n/30.

44. Feb 28: Total food sales from the week are shown in the table below:

Item	Quantity Sold	Sales Price	Totals
Bottled Water	5	$1.50	$7.50
Sports Drink:			
Lemon	4	2.00	8.00
Orange	2	2.00	4.00
Blue	3	2.00	6.00
Red		2.00	
Energy Drink:			
Regular		3.75	
Sugar-Free	5	3.75	18.75
Nutrition Bar:			
Chocolate	2	3.25	6.50
Vanilla	3	3.25	9.75
Peanut Butter	1	3.25	3.25
Subtotal			**63.75**
Sales Tax			**5.10**
Total			**68.85**

45. Feb 28: Deposited all Undeposited funds from the last week of the month into the checking account. Total Deposit is $228.85.

Reconcile Accounts

Use the following information to reconcile the checking account:

Bank Statement Ending Date	2/28/2013
Bank Statement Ending Balance	$117,673.88
Outstanding Checks:	Outstanding Deposits:
Check # 1018 $147.62	2/28/2013 $228.85
Check # 1019 $183.86	
Check # 1020 $51.45	
Check # 1021 $45.00	
Check # 1022 $126.48	

Checks and Payments

	Date	Type	Num	Name	Amount
✓	01/26/2013	Check	1008	ABC Web Designs	300.00
✓	01/28/2013	Check	1009	Val-Pak	225.00
✓	02/01/2013	Check	1010	Great American Bank	1,859.82
✓	02/01/2013	Check	1011	Oak Hill Homeowner's Association	150.00
✓	02/03/2013	Check	1012	Willy's Windows	75.00
✓	02/05/2013	Check	1013	Long for Success, LLC	450.00
✓	02/08/2013	Check	1014	Copper Property Management Co.	1,500.00
✓	02/15/2013	Bill Pay...	1015	Yoga Bliss, LLC	235.00
✓	02/15/2013	Refund	1016	Jim Hill	20.00
✓	02/25/2013	Bill Pay...	1017	Swisher Marketing, LLC	750.00
☐	02/28/2013	Bill Pay...	1018	Time Warner	147.62
☐	02/28/2013	Bill Pay...	1019	Metro Electric Co.	183.86
☐	02/28/2013	Bill Pay...	1020	City of Springfield	51.45
☐	02/28/2013	Bill Pay...	1021	Waste Management	45.00
☐	02/28/2013	Bill Pay...	1022	Fit Foods, Inc.	126.48

Use the following information to reconcile the Visa credit card account:

Bank Statement Ending Date	2/28/2013
Bank Statement Ending Balance	$68.97
Outstanding Items: Office Depot $56.70	

After reconciling the credit card account, select Write a check for payment now. Enter the payment date of Mar. 1 payable to Great American Bank for $68.97 with check number 1023.

Check Your Progress

Create the following reports and compare them to the following reports. (Make sure to change your dates for February only).

Balance Sheet

As of February 28, 2013

	Total
ASSETS	
Current Assets	
Bank Accounts	
Hometown Bank	117,348.32
Total Bank Accounts	**$117,348.32**
Accounts Receivable	
Accounts Receivable (A/R)	245.00
Total Accounts Receivable	**$ 245.00**
Other current assets	
Inventory Asset	93.14
Undeposited Funds	0.00
Total Other current assets	**$ 93.14**
Total Current Assets	**$117,686.46**
Fixed Assets	
Fitness Equipment	
Elliptical Machines	10,000.00
Free Weights	8,000.00
Stationary Bikes	12,000.00
Treadmills	10,000.00
Weight Machines	40,000.00
Total Fitness Equipment	**$ 80,000.00**
Leasehold Improvements	52,736.89
Office Furniture & Equipment	4,123.15
Outdoor Signage	1,200.00
Total Fixed Assets	**$138,060.04**
Other Assets	
Security Deposit	3,000.00
Total Other Assets	**$ 3,000.00**
TOTAL ASSETS	**$258,746.50**

LIABILITIES AND EQUITY

Liabilities		
Current Liabilities		
Accounts Payable		
Accounts Payable (A/P)		457.93
Total Accounts Payable	$	**457.93**
Credit Cards		
Visa		125.67
Total Credit Cards	$	**125.67**
Other Current Liabilities		
Iowa Department of Revenue Payable		11.44
Total Other Current Liabilities	$	**11.44**
Total Current Liabilities	$	**595.04**
Long-Term Liabilities		
Notes Payable - Hometown Bank		250,000.00
Total Long-Term Liabilities		**$250,000.00**
Total Liabilities		**$250,595.04**
Equity		
Joe Watson		
Joe Watson Partner Contribution		5,000.00
Total Joe Watson	$	**5,000.00**
Nancy Clemens		
Nancy Clemens Partner Contribution		5,000.00
Total Nancy Clemens	$	**5,000.00**
Opening Balance Equity		
Retained Earnings		
Tom Martin		
Tom Partner Contributions		5,000.00
Total Tom Martin	$	**5,000.00**
Net Income		-6,848.54
Total Equity	$	**8,151.46**
TOTAL LIABILITIES AND EQUITY		**$258,746.50**

Profit & Loss (Jan 01 - Feb 28)

To create a monthly Profit & Loss, go to Reports > Profit & Loss enter the dates and click on Customize and change columns to Months.

January - February, 2013

	Jan 2013	Feb 2013	Total
Income			
Gym Revenues		1,235.00	1,235.00
Registration Fees		175.00	175.00
Sales of Product Income		143.00	143.00
Total Income	$ 0.00	$ 1,553.00	$ 1,553.00
Cost of Goods Sold			
Cost of Goods Sold		27.04	27.04
Inventory Shrinkage		6.30	6.30
Total Cost of Goods Sold	$ 0.00	$ 33.34	$ 33.34
Gross Profit	$ 0.00	$ 1,519.66	$ 1,519.66
Expenses			
Advertising	225.00	900.00	1,125.00
Cleaning Supplies		68.97	68.97
computer & Internet	550.00		550.00
Fitness Supplies		235.00	235.00
Legal & Professional Fees	1,785.00		1,785.00
Accounting Fees		450.00	450.00
Total Legal & Professional Fees	$ 1,785.00	$ 450.00	$ 2,235.00
Office Expenses	136.67	56.70	193.37
Rent or Lease	1,500.00	1,500.00	3,000.00
Repair & Maintenance		75.00	75.00
Utilities			0.00
Electricity	183.86	178.86	362.72
Phone/Internet	147.62	147.62	295.24
Trash Removal	45.00	45.00	90.00
Water	51.45	86.45	137.90
Total Utilities	$ 427.93	$ 457.93	$ 885.86
Total Expenses	$ 4,624.60	$ 3,743.60	$ 8,368.20
Net Operating Income	-$ 4,624.60	-$ 2,223.94	-$ 6,848.54
Net Income	-$ 4,624.60	-$ 2,223.94	-$ 6,848.54

Accounts Receivable Aging Detail

As of February 28, 2013

	Date	Transaction Type	Num	Client	Due Date	Amount	Open Balance
Current							
	02/22/2013	Invoice	1029	Cindy Blackburn	03/24/2013	35.00	35.00
	02/22/2013	Invoice	1028	Robert Markum	03/24/2013	35.00	35.00
	02/22/2013	Invoice	1027	Tim Barnes	03/24/2013	35.00	35.00
	02/22/2013	Invoice	1023	Daniel Brown	03/24/2013	35.00	35.00
	02/22/2013	Invoice	1025	Lucy Steele	03/24/2013	35.00	35.00
	02/22/2013	Invoice	1024	Adrian Gonzalez	03/24/2013	35.00	35.00
	02/22/2013	Invoice	1026	Jerry Kline	03/24/2013	35.00	35.00
Total for Current						245.00	245.00
TOTAL						245.00	245.00

Accounts Payable Aging Detail

As of February 28, 2013

	Date	Transaction Type	Vendor	Due Date	Amount	Open Balance
Current						
	02/28/2013	Bill	Waste Management	03/30/2013	45.00	45.00
	02/28/2013	Bill	Time Warner	03/30/2013	147.62	147.62
	02/28/2013	Bill	Metro Electric Co.	03/30/2013	178.86	178.86
	02/28/2013	Bill	City of Springfield	03/30/2013	86.45	86.45
Total for Current					457.93	457.93
TOTAL					457.93	457.93

Sales by Customer Detail

February 2013

	Date	Transaction Type	Num	Product/Service	Qty	Rate	Amount
Adrian Gonzalez							
	02/06/2013	Invoice	1005	Monthly Membership	1.00	35.00	35.00
	02/07/2013	Sales Receipt	1009	Basic Fitness 101	1.00	50.00	50.00
	02/10/2013	Sales Receipt	1017	Personal Training	1.00	35.00	35.00
	02/22/2013	Invoice	1024	Monthly Membership	1.00	35.00	35.00
	02/23/2013	Sales Receipt	1031	Personal Training	2.00	35.00	70.00
Total for Adrian Gonzalez							**225.00**
Augusto Gutierrez							
	02/04/2013	Sales Receipt	1004	Quarterly	1.00	90.00	90.00
Total for Augusto Gutierrez							**90.00**
Christopher Tomlinson							
	02/20/2013	Sales Receipt	1021	Monthly Membership	1.00	35.00	35.00
	02/20/2013	Sales Receipt	1021	Registration Fees	1.00	25.00	25.00
Total for Christopher Tomlinson							**60.00**
Cindy Blackburn							
	02/16/2013	Sales Receipt	1020	Registration Fees	1.00	25.00	25.00
	02/16/2013	Sales Receipt	1020	Monthly Membership	1.00	35.00	35.00
	02/22/2013	Invoice	1029	Monthly Membership	1.00	35.00	35.00
Total for Cindy Blackburn							**95.00**
Daniel Brown							
	02/06/2013	Invoice	1006	Monthly Membership	1.00	35.00	35.00
	02/07/2013	Sales Receipt	1011	Wicked Weights	1.00	50.00	50.00
	02/22/2013	Invoice	1023	Monthly Membership	1.00	35.00	35.00
Total for Daniel Brown							**120.00**
Jerry Kline							
	02/04/2013	Sales Receipt	1002	Registration Fees	1.00	25.00	25.00
	02/04/2013	Sales Receipt	1002	Monthly Membership	1.00	35.00	35.00
	02/07/2013	Sales Receipt	1008	Basic Fitness 101	1.00	50.00	50.00
	02/22/2013	Invoice	1026	Monthly Membership	1.00	35.00	35.00
Total for Jerry Kline							**145.00**
Jim Hill							
	02/04/2013	Sales Receipt	1003	Monthly Membership	1.00	35.00	35.00
	02/04/2013	Sales Receipt	1003	Registration Fees	1.00	25.00	25.00
	02/07/2013	Sales Receipt	1012	Wicked Weights	1.00	50.00	50.00
	02/15/2013	Refund	1020	Monthly Membership	-1.00	20.00	-20.00
Total for Jim Hill							**90.00**
Julie Stein							
	02/14/2013	Sales Receipt	1018	Quarterly	1.00	90.00	90.00
Total for Julie Stein							**90.00**
Lucy Hopper							
	02/06/2013	Invoice	1007	Monthly Membership	1.00	35.00	35.00
Total for Lucy Hopper							**35.00**
Lucy Steele							
	02/04/2013	Sales Receipt	1001	Monthly Membership	1.00	35.00	35.00

MICHELLE L. LONG AND ANDREW S. LONG

		02/04/2013	Sales Receipt	1001	Registration Fees	1.00	25.00	25.00
		02/07/2013	Sales Receipt	1010	Basic Fitness 101	1.00	50.00	50.00
		02/22/2013	Invoice	1025	Monthly Membership	1.00	35.00	35.00
Total for Lucy Steele								**145.00**
Lynn Sampson								
		02/23/2013	Sales Receipt	1030	Quarterly	1.00	90.00	90.00
Total for Lynn Sampson								**90.00**
Robert Markum								
		02/10/2013	Sales Receipt	1016	Registration Fees	1.00	25.00	25.00
		02/10/2013	Sales Receipt	1016	Monthly Membership	1.00	35.00	35.00
		02/22/2013	Invoice	1028	Monthly Membership	1.00	35.00	35.00
Total for Robert Markum								**95.00**
Tim Barnes								
		02/07/2013	Sales Receipt	1013	Registration Fees	1.00	25.00	25.00
		02/07/2013	Sales Receipt	1013	Monthly Membership	1.00	35.00	35.00
		02/07/2013	Sales Receipt	1014	Personal Training	1.00	35.00	35.00
		02/22/2013	Invoice	1027	Monthly Membership	1.00	35.00	35.00
Total for Tim Barnes								**130.00**
Weekly Sales								
		02/07/2013	Sales Receipt	1015	Nutrition Bar:Chocolate	-1.00	0.45	-0.45
		02/07/2013	Sales Receipt	1015	Sports Drink:Blue Drink	-2.00	0.37	-0.74
		02/07/2013	Sales Receipt	1015	Sports Drink:Orange Drink	-2.00	0.37	-0.74
		02/07/2013	Sales Receipt	1015	Sports Drink:Blue Drink	2.00	0.37	0.74
		02/07/2013	Sales Receipt	1015	Nutrition Bar:Chocolate	1.00	0.45	0.45
		02/07/2013	Sales Receipt	1015	Nutrition Bar:Chocolate	1.00	3.25	3.25
		02/07/2013	Sales Receipt	1015	Sports Drink:Orange Drink	2.00	2.00	4.00
		02/07/2013	Sales Receipt	1015	Sports Drink:Blue Drink	2.00	2.00	4.00
		02/07/2013	Sales Receipt	1015	Sports Drink:Orange Drink	2.00	0.37	0.74
		02/14/2013	Sales Receipt	1019	Sports Drink:Red Drink	1.00	2.00	2.00
		02/14/2013	Sales Receipt	1019	Sports Drink:Blue Drink	2.00	2.00	4.00
		02/14/2013	Sales Receipt	1019	Sports Drink:Lemon	3.00	2.00	6.00
		02/14/2013	Sales Receipt	1019	Energy Drink:Sugar-Free	2.00	3.75	7.50
		02/14/2013	Sales Receipt	1019	Nutrition Bar:Chocolate	3.00	3.25	9.75
		02/14/2013	Sales Receipt	1019	Energy Drink:Sugar-Free	-2.00	1.05	-2.10
		02/14/2013	Sales Receipt	1019	Sports Drink:Red Drink	1.00	0.37	0.37
		02/14/2013	Sales Receipt	1019	Sports Drink:Blue Drink	2.00	0.37	0.74
		02/14/2013	Sales Receipt	1019	Sports Drink:Lemon	3.00	0.37	1.11
		02/14/2013	Sales Receipt	1019	Nutrition Bar:Chocolate	3.00	0.45	1.35
		02/14/2013	Sales Receipt	1019	Energy Drink:Sugar-Free	2.00	1.05	2.10
		02/14/2013	Sales Receipt	1019	Nutrition Bar:Chocolate	-3.00	0.45	-1.35
		02/14/2013	Sales Receipt	1019	Sports Drink:Lemon	-3.00	0.37	-1.11
		02/14/2013	Sales Receipt	1019	Sports Drink:Blue Drink	-2.00	0.37	-0.74
		02/14/2013	Sales Receipt	1019	Sports Drink:Red Drink	-1.00	0.37	-0.37
		02/21/2013	Sales Receipt	1022	Nutrition Bar:Chocolate	-1.00	0.45	-0.45
		02/21/2013	Sales Receipt	1022	Sports Drink:Orange Drink	1.00	2.00	2.00
		02/21/2013	Sales Receipt	1022	Bottled Water	-3.00	0.17	-0.51
		02/21/2013	Sales Receipt	1022	Nutrition Bar:Vanilla Bar	-2.00	0.45	-0.90
		02/21/2013	Sales Receipt	1022	Sports Drink:Blue Drink	-4.00	0.37	-1.48
		02/21/2013	Sales Receipt	1022	Energy Drink:Sugar-Free	-3.00	1.05	-3.15

Date	Type	Num	Item	Qty	Rate	Amount
02/21/2013	Sales Receipt	1022	Nutrition Bar:Vanilla Bar	2.00	3.25	6.50
02/21/2013	Sales Receipt	1022	Sports Drink:Blue Drink	4.00	2.00	8.00
02/21/2013	Sales Receipt	1022	Energy Drink:Sugar-Free	3.00	3.75	11.25
02/21/2013	Sales Receipt	1022	Sports Drink:Blue Drink	4.00	0.37	1.48
02/21/2013	Sales Receipt	1022	Nutrition Bar:Vanilla Bar	2.00	0.45	0.90
02/21/2013	Sales Receipt	1022	Sports Drink:Orange Drink	-1.00	0.37	-0.37
02/21/2013	Sales Receipt	1022	Sports Drink:Orange Drink	1.00	0.37	0.37
02/21/2013	Sales Receipt	1022	Energy Drink:Sugar-Free	3.00	1.05	3.15
02/21/2013	Sales Receipt	1022	Nutrition Bar:Peanut Butter Bar	1.00	0.45	0.45
02/21/2013	Sales Receipt	1022	Nutrition Bar:Chocolate	1.00	0.45	0.45
02/21/2013	Sales Receipt	1022	Bottled Water	3.00	0.17	0.51
02/21/2013	Sales Receipt	1022	Bottled Water	3.00	1.50	4.50
02/21/2013	Sales Receipt	1022	Nutrition Bar:Peanut Butter Bar	1.00	3.25	3.25
02/21/2013	Sales Receipt	1022	Nutrition Bar:Chocolate	1.00	3.25	3.25
02/21/2013	Sales Receipt	1022	Nutrition Bar:Peanut Butter Bar	-1.00	0.45	-0.45
02/28/2013	Sales Receipt	1032	Energy Drink:Sugar-Free	5.00	3.75	18.75
02/28/2013	Sales Receipt	1032	Nutrition Bar:Vanilla Bar	3.00	3.25	9.75
02/28/2013	Sales Receipt	1032	Sports Drink:Lemon	4.00	2.00	8.00
02/28/2013	Sales Receipt	1032	Bottled Water	5.00	1.50	7.50
02/28/2013	Sales Receipt	1032	Nutrition Bar:Chocolate	2.00	3.25	6.50
02/28/2013	Sales Receipt	1032	Sports Drink:Blue Drink	3.00	2.00	6.00
02/28/2013	Sales Receipt	1032	Sports Drink:Orange Drink	2.00	2.00	4.00
02/28/2013	Sales Receipt	1032	Nutrition Bar:Peanut Butter Bar	1.00	3.25	3.25
02/28/2013	Sales Receipt	1032	Nutrition Bar:Peanut Butter Bar	-1.00	0.45	-0.45
02/28/2013	Sales Receipt	1032	Sports Drink:Orange Drink	-2.00	0.37	-0.74
02/28/2013	Sales Receipt	1032	Bottled Water	-5.00	0.17	-0.85
02/28/2013	Sales Receipt	1032	Nutrition Bar:Chocolate	-2.00	0.45	-0.90
02/28/2013	Sales Receipt	1032	Sports Drink:Blue Drink	-3.00	0.37	-1.11
02/28/2013	Sales Receipt	1032	Nutrition Bar:Vanilla Bar	-3.00	0.45	-1.35
02/28/2013	Sales Receipt	1032	Sports Drink:Lemon	-4.00	0.37	-1.48
02/28/2013	Sales Receipt	1032	Energy Drink:Sugar-Free	-5.00	1.05	-5.25
02/28/2013	Sales Receipt	1032	Energy Drink:Sugar-Free	5.00	1.05	5.25
02/28/2013	Sales Receipt	1032	Sports Drink:Lemon	4.00	0.37	1.48
02/28/2013	Sales Receipt	1032	Nutrition Bar:Vanilla Bar	3.00	0.45	1.35
02/28/2013	Sales Receipt	1032	Sports Drink:Blue Drink	3.00	0.37	1.11
02/28/2013	Sales Receipt	1032	Nutrition Bar:Chocolate	2.00	0.45	0.90
02/28/2013	Sales Receipt	1032	Bottled Water	5.00	0.17	0.85
02/28/2013	Sales Receipt	1032	Sports Drink:Orange Drink	2.00	0.37	0.74
02/28/2013	Sales Receipt	1032	Nutrition Bar:Peanut Butter Bar	1.00	0.45	0.45

Total for Weekly Sales   **143.00**

TOTAL   **1,553.00**

Sales by Product/Service Detail

February 2013

	Date	Transaction Type	Num	Client	Qty	Rate	Amount
Basic Fitness 101							
	02/07/2013	Sales Receipt	1010	Lucy Steele	1.00	50.00	50.00
	02/07/2013	Sales Receipt	1008	Jerry Kline	1.00	50.00	50.00
	02/07/2013	Sales Receipt	1009	Adrian Gonzalez	1.00	50.00	50.00
Total for Basic Fitness 101							**150.00**
Bottled Water							
	02/21/2013	Sales Receipt	1022	Weekly Sales	-3.00	0.17	-0.51
	02/21/2013	Sales Receipt	1022	Weekly Sales	3.00	1.50	4.50
	02/21/2013	Sales Receipt	1022	Weekly Sales	3.00	0.17	0.51
	02/28/2013	Sales Receipt	1032	Weekly Sales	5.00	1.50	7.50
	02/28/2013	Sales Receipt	1032	Weekly Sales	5.00	0.17	0.85
	02/28/2013	Sales Receipt	1032	Weekly Sales	-5.00	0.17	-0.85
Total for Bottled Water							**12.00**
Energy Drink							
Sugar-Free							
	02/14/2013	Sales Receipt	1019	Weekly Sales	-2.00	1.05	-2.10
	02/14/2013	Sales Receipt	1019	Weekly Sales	2.00	1.05	2.10
	02/14/2013	Sales Receipt	1019	Weekly Sales	2.00	3.75	7.50
	02/21/2013	Sales Receipt	1022	Weekly Sales	-3.00	1.05	-3.15
	02/21/2013	Sales Receipt	1022	Weekly Sales	3.00	1.05	3.15
	02/21/2013	Sales Receipt	1022	Weekly Sales	3.00	3.75	11.25
	02/28/2013	Sales Receipt	1032	Weekly Sales	5.00	1.05	5.25
	02/28/2013	Sales Receipt	1032	Weekly Sales	5.00	3.75	18.75
	02/28/2013	Sales Receipt	1032	Weekly Sales	-5.00	1.05	-5.25
Total for Sugar-Free							**37.50**
Total for Energy Drink							**37.50**
Monthly Membership							
	02/04/2013	Sales Receipt	1003	Jim Hill	1.00	35.00	35.00
	02/04/2013	Sales Receipt	1001	Lucy Steele	1.00	35.00	35.00
	02/04/2013	Sales Receipt	1002	Jerry Kline	1.00	35.00	35.00
	02/06/2013	Invoice	1005	Adrian Gonzalez	1.00	35.00	35.00
	02/06/2013	Invoice	1006	Daniel Brown	1.00	35.00	35.00
	02/06/2013	Invoice	1007	Lucy Hopper	1.00	35.00	35.00
	02/07/2013	Sales Receipt	1013	Tim Barnes	1.00	35.00	35.00
	02/10/2013	Sales Receipt	1016	Robert Markum	1.00	35.00	35.00
	02/15/2013	Refund	1020	Jim Hill	-1.00	20.00	-20.00
	02/16/2013	Sales Receipt	1020	Cindy Blackburn	1.00	35.00	35.00
	02/20/2013	Sales Receipt	1021	Christopher Tomlinson	1.00	35.00	35.00
	02/22/2013	Invoice	1024	Adrian Gonzalez	1.00	35.00	35.00
	02/22/2013	Invoice	1025	Lucy Steele	1.00	35.00	35.00
	02/22/2013	Invoice	1026	Jerry Kline	1.00	35.00	35.00
	02/22/2013	Invoice	1027	Tim Barnes	1.00	35.00	35.00
	02/22/2013	Invoice	1028	Robert Markum	1.00	35.00	35.00
	02/22/2013	Invoice	1029	Cindy Blackburn	1.00	35.00	35.00
	02/22/2013	Invoice	1023	Daniel Brown	1.00	35.00	35.00
Total for Monthly Membership							**575.00**

Nutrition Bar
   Chocolate

	02/07/2013	Sales Receipt	1015	Weekly Sales	-1.00	0.45	-0.45
	02/07/2013	Sales Receipt	1015	Weekly Sales	1.00	0.45	0.45
	02/07/2013	Sales Receipt	1015	Weekly Sales	1.00	3.25	3.25
	02/14/2013	Sales Receipt	1019	Weekly Sales	-3.00	0.45	-1.35
	02/14/2013	Sales Receipt	1019	Weekly Sales	3.00	3.25	9.75
	02/14/2013	Sales Receipt	1019	Weekly Sales	3.00	0.45	1.35
	02/21/2013	Sales Receipt	1022	Weekly Sales	1.00	3.25	3.25
	02/21/2013	Sales Receipt	1022	Weekly Sales	1.00	0.45	0.45
	02/21/2013	Sales Receipt	1022	Weekly Sales	-1.00	0.45	-0.45
	02/28/2013	Sales Receipt	1032	Weekly Sales	2.00	3.25	6.50
	02/28/2013	Sales Receipt	1032	Weekly Sales	2.00	0.45	0.90
	02/28/2013	Sales Receipt	1032	Weekly Sales	-2.00	0.45	-0.90

Total for Chocolate   **22.75**

   Peanut Butter Bar

	02/21/2013	Sales Receipt	1022	Weekly Sales	1.00	0.45	0.45
	02/21/2013	Sales Receipt	1022	Weekly Sales	1.00	3.25	3.25
	02/21/2013	Sales Receipt	1022	Weekly Sales	-1.00	0.45	-0.45
	02/28/2013	Sales Receipt	1032	Weekly Sales	1.00	0.45	0.45
	02/28/2013	Sales Receipt	1032	Weekly Sales	1.00	3.25	3.25
	02/28/2013	Sales Receipt	1032	Weekly Sales	-1.00	0.45	-0.45

Total for Peanut Butter Bar   **6.50**

   Vanilla Bar

	02/21/2013	Sales Receipt	1022	Weekly Sales	2.00	0.45	0.90
	02/21/2013	Sales Receipt	1022	Weekly Sales	-2.00	0.45	-0.90
	02/21/2013	Sales Receipt	1022	Weekly Sales	2.00	3.25	6.50
	02/28/2013	Sales Receipt	1032	Weekly Sales	3.00	3.25	9.75
	02/28/2013	Sales Receipt	1032	Weekly Sales	-3.00	0.45	-1.35
	02/28/2013	Sales Receipt	1032	Weekly Sales	3.00	0.45	1.35

Total for Vanilla Bar   **16.25**

Total for Nutrition Bar   **45.50**

Personal Training

	02/07/2013	Sales Receipt	1014	Tim Barnes	1.00	35.00	35.00
	02/10/2013	Sales Receipt	1017	Adrian Gonzalez	1.00	35.00	35.00
	02/23/2013	Sales Receipt	1031	Adrian Gonzalez	2.00	35.00	70.00

Total for Personal Training   **140.00**

Quarterly

	02/04/2013	Sales Receipt	1004	Augusto Gutierrez	1.00	90.00	90.00
	02/14/2013	Sales Receipt	1018	Julie Stein	1.00	90.00	90.00
	02/23/2013	Sales Receipt	1030	Lynn Sampson	1.00	90.00	90.00

Total for Quarterly   **270.00**

Registration Fees

	02/04/2013	Sales Receipt	1003	Jim Hill	1.00	25.00	25.00
	02/04/2013	Sales Receipt	1001	Lucy Steele	1.00	25.00	25.00
	02/04/2013	Sales Receipt	1002	Jerry Kline	1.00	25.00	25.00
	02/07/2013	Sales Receipt	1013	Tim Barnes	1.00	25.00	25.00
	02/10/2013	Sales Receipt	1016	Robert Markum	1.00	25.00	25.00

MICHELLE L. LONG AND ANDREW S. LONG

	02/16/2013	Sales Receipt	1020	Cindy Blackburn	1.00	25.00	25.00
	02/20/2013	Sales Receipt	1021	Christopher Tomlinson	1.00	25.00	25.00

Total for Registration Fees **175.00**

Sports Drink
  Blue Drink

02/07/2013	Sales Receipt	1015	Weekly Sales	2.00	0.37	0.74
02/07/2013	Sales Receipt	1015	Weekly Sales	2.00	2.00	4.00
02/07/2013	Sales Receipt	1015	Weekly Sales	-2.00	0.37	-0.74
02/14/2013	Sales Receipt	1019	Weekly Sales	2.00	2.00	4.00
02/14/2013	Sales Receipt	1019	Weekly Sales	-2.00	0.37	-0.74
02/14/2013	Sales Receipt	1019	Weekly Sales	2.00	0.37	0.74
02/21/2013	Sales Receipt	1022	Weekly Sales	4.00	2.00	8.00
02/21/2013	Sales Receipt	1022	Weekly Sales	-4.00	0.37	-1.48
02/21/2013	Sales Receipt	1022	Weekly Sales	4.00	0.37	1.48
02/28/2013	Sales Receipt	1032	Weekly Sales	3.00	0.37	1.11
02/28/2013	Sales Receipt	1032	Weekly Sales	-3.00	0.37	-1.11
02/28/2013	Sales Receipt	1032	Weekly Sales	3.00	2.00	6.00

Total for Blue Drink **22.00**

Lemon

02/14/2013	Sales Receipt	1019	Weekly Sales	3.00	0.37	1.11
02/14/2013	Sales Receipt	1019	Weekly Sales	3.00	2.00	6.00
02/14/2013	Sales Receipt	1019	Weekly Sales	-3.00	0.37	-1.11
02/28/2013	Sales Receipt	1032	Weekly Sales	-4.00	0.37	-1.48
02/28/2013	Sales Receipt	1032	Weekly Sales	4.00	0.37	1.48
02/28/2013	Sales Receipt	1032	Weekly Sales	4.00	2.00	8.00

Total for Lemon **14.00**

Orange Drink

02/07/2013	Sales Receipt	1015	Weekly Sales	-2.00	0.37	-0.74
02/07/2013	Sales Receipt	1015	Weekly Sales	2.00	0.37	0.74
02/07/2013	Sales Receipt	1015	Weekly Sales	2.00	2.00	4.00
02/21/2013	Sales Receipt	1022	Weekly Sales	1.00	2.00	2.00
02/21/2013	Sales Receipt	1022	Weekly Sales	-1.00	0.37	-0.37
02/21/2013	Sales Receipt	1022	Weekly Sales	1.00	0.37	0.37
02/28/2013	Sales Receipt	1032	Weekly Sales	-2.00	0.37	-0.74
02/28/2013	Sales Receipt	1032	Weekly Sales	2.00	0.37	0.74
02/28/2013	Sales Receipt	1032	Weekly Sales	2.00	2.00	4.00

Total for Orange Drink **10.00**

Red Drink

02/14/2013	Sales Receipt	1019	Weekly Sales	1.00	2.00	2.00
02/14/2013	Sales Receipt	1019	Weekly Sales	1.00	0.37	0.37
02/14/2013	Sales Receipt	1019	Weekly Sales	-1.00	0.37	-0.37

Total for Red Drink **2.00**
Total for Sports Drink **48.00**

Wicked Weights

02/07/2013	Sales Receipt	1012	Jim Hill	1.00	50.00	50.00
02/07/2013	Sales Receipt	1011	Daniel Brown	1.00	50.00	50.00

Total for Wicked Weights **100.00**
TOTAL **1,553.00**

Inventory Valuation Summary

As of February 28, 2013

	Total		
	Qty	Asset Value	Avg Cost
Bottled Water	40.00	6.80	0.17
Energy Drink			
Regular	24.00	25.20	1.05
Sugar-Free	8.00	8.40	1.05
Total Energy Drink		$ 33.60	
Nutrition Bar			
Chocolate	17.00	7.65	0.45
Peanut Butter Bar	22.00	9.90	0.45
Vanilla Bar	19.00	8.55	0.45
Total Nutrition Bar		$ 26.10	
Sports Drink			
Blue Drink	13.00	4.81	0.37
Lemon	17.00	6.29	0.37
Orange Drink	19.00	7.03	0.37
Red Drink	23.00	8.51	0.37
Total Sports Drink		$ 26.64	
TOTAL		$ 93.14	

Income List

To access the Income List, go to Customers > Income List

All transactions from All Dates

Date	Type	Num	Name	Due Date	Amount Due	Total	Status
2013-02-04	Sales Receipt	1001	Lucy Steele		0.00	60.00	Paid
2013-02-04	Sales Receipt	1002	Jerry Kline		0.00	60.00	Paid
2013-02-04	Sales Receipt	1003	Jim Hill		0.00	60.00	Paid
2013-02-04	Sales Receipt	1004	Augusto Gutierrez		0.00	90.00	Paid
2013-02-06	Invoice	1005	Adrian Gonzalez	2013-02-16	0.00	35.00	Paid
2013-02-06	Invoice	1006	Daniel Brown	2013-02-16	0.00	35.00	Paid
2013-02-06	Invoice	1007	Lucy Hopper	2013-02-16	0.00	35.00	Paid
2013-02-07	Sales Receipt	1008	Jerry Kline		0.00	50.00	Paid
2013-02-07	Sales Receipt	1009	Adrian Gonzalez		0.00	50.00	Paid
2013-02-07	Sales Receipt	1010	Lucy Steele		0.00	50.00	Paid
2013-02-07	Sales Receipt	1011	Daniel Brown		0.00	50.00	Paid
2013-02-07	Sales Receipt	1012	Jim Hill		0.00	50.00	Paid
2013-02-07	Sales Receipt	1013	Tim Barnes		0.00	60.00	Paid
2013-02-07	Sales Receipt	1014	Tim Barnes		0.00	35.00	Paid
2013-02-07	Sales Receipt	1015	Weekly Sales		0.00	12.15	Paid
2013-02-10	Sales Receipt	1016	Robert Markum		0.00	60.00	Paid
2013-02-10	Sales Receipt	1017	Adrian Gonzalez		0.00	35.00	Paid
2013-02-14	Sales Receipt	1018	Julie Stein		0.00	90.00	Paid
2013-02-14	Sales Receipt	1019	Weekly Sales		0.00	31.59	Paid
2013-02-16	Sales Receipt	1020	Cindy Blackburn		0.00	60.00	Paid
2013-02-20	Sales Receipt	1021	Christopher Tomlinson		0.00	60.00	Paid
2013-02-21	Sales Receipt	1022	Weekly Sales		0.00	41.85	Paid
2013-02-22	Invoice	1023	Daniel Brown	2013-03-24	35.00	35.00	Overdue
2013-02-22	Invoice	1024	Adrian Gonzalez	2013-03-24	35.00	35.00	Overdue
2013-02-22	Invoice	1025	Lucy Steele	2013-03-24	35.00	35.00	Overdue
2013-02-22	Invoice	1026	Jerry Kline	2013-03-24	35.00	35.00	Overdue
2013-02-22	Invoice	1027	Tim Barnes	2013-03-24	35.00	35.00	Overdue
2013-02-22	Invoice	1028	Robert Markum	2013-03-24	35.00	35.00	Overdue
2013-02-22	Invoice	1029	Cindy Blackburn	2013-03-24	35.00	35.00	Overdue
2013-02-23	Sales Receipt	1030	Lynn Sampson		0.00	90.00	Paid
2013-02-23	Sales Receipt	1031	Adrian Gonzalez		0.00	70.00	Paid
2013-02-28	Sales Receipt	1032	Weekly Sales		0.00	68.85	Paid

Transaction List by Date

Date	Transaction Type	Num	Name	Account	Split	Amount
02/01/2013	Check	1010	Great American Bank	Hometown Bank	Visa	-1,859.82
02/01/2013	Check	1011	Oak Hill Homeowner's Association	Hometown Bank	Advertising	-150.00
02/03/2013	Check	1012	Willy's Windows	Hometown Bank	Repair & Maintenance	-75.00
02/03/2013	Bill		Fit Foods, Inc.	Accounts Payable (A/P)	-Split-	126.48
02/04/2013	Sales Receipt	1001	Lucy Steele	Undeposited Funds	-Split-	60.00
02/04/2013	Sales Receipt	1002	Jerry Kline	Undeposited Funds	-Split-	60.00
02/04/2013	Bill		Yoga Bliss, LLC	Accounts Payable (A/P)	Fitness Supplies	235.00
02/04/2013	Sales Receipt	1003	Jim Hill	Undeposited Funds	-Split-	60.00
02/04/2013	Sales Receipt	1004	Augusto Gutierrez	Undeposited Funds	Gym Revenues	90.00
02/05/2013	Check	1013	Long for Success, LLC	Hometown Bank	Legal & Professional Fees:Accounting Fees	-450.00
02/06/2013	Invoice	1005	Adrian Gonzalez	Accounts Receivable (A/R)	Gym Revenues	35.00
02/06/2013	Invoice	1006	Daniel Brown	Accounts Receivable (A/R)	Gym Revenues	35.00
02/06/2013	Invoice	1007	Lucy Hopper	Accounts Receivable (A/R)	Gym Revenues	35.00
02/07/2013	Sales Receipt	1008	Jerry Kline	Undeposited Funds	Gym Revenues	50.00
02/07/2013	Sales Receipt	1009	Adrian Gonzalez	Undeposited Funds	Gym Revenues	50.00
02/07/2013	Sales Receipt	1010	Lucy Steele	Undeposited Funds	Gym Revenues	50.00
02/07/2013	Sales Receipt	1011	Daniel Brown	Undeposited Funds	Gym Revenues	50.00
02/07/2013	Sales Receipt	1012	Jim Hill	Undeposited Funds	Gym Revenues	50.00
02/07/2013	Sales Receipt	1013	Tim Barnes	Undeposited Funds	-Split-	60.00
02/07/2013	Sales Receipt	1014	Tim Barnes	Undeposited Funds	Gym Revenues	35.00
02/07/2013	Payment		Adrian Gonzalez	Undeposited Funds	Accounts Receivable (A/R)	35.00
02/07/2013	Sales Receipt	1015	Weekly Sales	Undeposited Funds	-Split-	12.15
02/07/2013	Deposit			Hometown Bank	-Split-	662.15
02/08/2013	Inventory Qty Adjust	1		Inventory Shrinkage	Inventory Asset	
02/08/2013	Check	1014	Copper Property Management Co.	Hometown Bank	Rent or Lease	-1,500.00
02/10/2013	Sales Receipt	1016	Robert Markum	Undeposited Funds	-Split-	60.00
02/10/2013	Sales Receipt	1017	Adrian Gonzalez	Undeposited Funds	Gym Revenues	35.00
02/11/2013	Payment		Lucy Hopper	Undeposited Funds	Accounts Receivable (A/R)	35.00
02/12/2013	Credit Card Expense		Wal-mart	Visa	Cleaning Supplies	68.97
02/14/2013	Sales Receipt	1018	Julie Stein	Undeposited Funds	Gym Revenues	90.00
02/14/2013	Sales Receipt	1019	Weekly Sales	Undeposited Funds	-Split-	31.59
02/14/2013	Deposit			Hometown Bank	-Split-	251.59
02/14/2013	Payment		Daniel Brown	Undeposited Funds	Accounts Receivable (A/R)	35.00
02/15/2013	Bill Payment (Check)	1015	Yoga Bliss, LLC	Hometown Bank	Accounts Payable (A/P)	-235.00
02/15/2013	Refund	1020	Jim Hill	Hometown Bank	Gym Revenues	-20.00
02/16/2013	Sales Receipt	1020	Cindy Blackburn	Undeposited Funds	-Split-	60.00
02/18/2013	Bill		Swisher Marketing, LLC	Accounts Payable (A/P)	Advertising	750.00
02/20/2013	Sales Receipt	1021	Christopher Tomlinson	Undeposited Funds	-Split-	60.00
02/21/2013	Sales Receipt	1022	Weekly Sales	Undeposited Funds	-Split-	41.85
02/21/2013	Deposit			Hometown Bank	-Split-	196.85

Date	Type	Num	Name	Account	Split	Amount
02/22/2013	Invoice	1023	Daniel Brown	Accounts Receivable (A/R)	Gym Revenues	35.00
02/22/2013	Invoice	1024	Adrian Gonzalez	Accounts Receivable (A/R)	Gym Revenues	35.00
02/22/2013	Invoice	1025	Lucy Steele	Accounts Receivable (A/R)	Gym Revenues	35.00
02/22/2013	Invoice	1026	Jerry Kline	Accounts Receivable (A/R)	Gym Revenues	35.00
02/22/2013	Invoice	1027	Tim Barnes	Accounts Receivable (A/R)	Gym Revenues	35.00
02/22/2013	Invoice	1028	Robert Markum	Accounts Receivable (A/R)	Gym Revenues	35.00
02/22/2013	Invoice	1029	Cindy Blackburn	Accounts Receivable (A/R)	Gym Revenues	35.00
02/23/2013	Sales Receipt	1030	Lynn Sampson	Undeposited Funds	Gym Revenues	90.00
02/23/2013	Sales Receipt	1031	Adrian Gonzalez	Undeposited Funds	Gym Revenues	70.00
02/25/2013	Bill Payment (Check)	1017	Swisher Marketing, LLC	Hometown Bank	Accounts Payable (A/P)	-750.00
02/26/2013	Credit Card Expense		Office Depot	Visa	Office Expenses	56.70
02/28/2013	Bill Payment (Check)	1018	Time Warner	Hometown Bank	Accounts Payable (A/P)	-147.62
02/28/2013	Bill Payment (Check)	1019	Metro Electric Co.	Hometown Bank	Accounts Payable (A/P)	-183.86
02/28/2013	Bill Payment (Check)	1020	City of Springfield	Hometown Bank	Accounts Payable (A/P)	-51.45
02/28/2013	Bill Payment (Check)	1021	Waste Management	Hometown Bank	Accounts Payable (A/P)	-45.00
02/28/2013	Bill Payment (Check)	1022	Fit Foods, Inc.	Hometown Bank	Accounts Payable (A/P)	-126.48
02/28/2013	Bill		Time Warner	Accounts Payable (A/P)	Utilities:Phone/Internet	147.62
02/28/2013	Bill		Metro Electric Co.	Accounts Payable (A/P)	Utilities:Electricity	178.86
02/28/2013	Bill		City of Springfield	Accounts Payable (A/P)	Utilities:Water	86.45
02/28/2013	Bill		Waste Management	Accounts Payable (A/P)	Utilities:Trash Removal	45.00
02/28/2013	Sales Receipt	1032	Weekly Sales	Undeposited Funds	-Split-	68.85
02/28/2013	Deposit			Hometown Bank	-Split-	228.85

5 ENTERING TRANSACTIONS – MARCH

Notes for entering transactions:

- Use Accounts Payable (i.e. Enter Bills and Pay Bills) for monthly expenses and bills (when transactions say Received Bill and Pay Bills).

- Enter Checks as indicated for purchases from local retailers and others.

- Use a Sales Receipt for initial registration fees and membership dues received. Subsequent membership dues will be entered as an Invoice and then Receive Payment.

- Enter Sales Receipts for classes and personal training sessions.

- The default in QuickBooks Online should be for payments received to go to Undeposited Funds -- you will be told when to Record Deposits.

- Do not worry about depreciation on fixed assets. We assumed the accountant or tax professional maintains details of fixed assets and depreciation.

March Transactions

1. Mar 1: Jules Silverstein paid $90 for a quarterly gym membership.

2. Mar 1: Sold 1 hour of personal training to Lynn Sampson for $35.

3. Mar 2: Received bill from Cool T-shirts Co. in the amount of $45.00 for custom staff t-shirts (set up a new expense account called uniforms, detail type office/general administrative), with terms of n/10.

4. Mar 3: Jim Dean paid $90 for a quarterly membership and 1 hour of personal training for $35 (Total Sales Receipt of $125).

5. Mar 3: Allison Hoch paid $90 for a quarterly gym membership.

6. Mar 3: Katie Layton paid $25 for a first time gym registration fee and a monthly membership fee of $35.

7. Mar 4: Received payment of $35 from Lucy Steele for March gym membership.

8. Mar 4: Recorded inventory adjustment: Fitness Haven, LLC gave out 1 free water to the first 10 customers. (Go to the Product / Service List, edit Bottled Water to Update the quantity on hand – enter the correct date and difference of -10).

9. Mar 4: Hugo Reyson paid $90 for a quarterly gym membership.

10. Mar 6: Check #1024 to Copper Property Management Co. in the amount of $1,500.00 for March rent.

11. Mar 7: The following table lists the members who signed up and paid (Sales Receipts) for March fitness classes. All classes are $50.

Basic Fitness 101	Wicked Weights	Kardio Killers	Yoga Fitness
Allison Hoch	John Brown	Jerry Kline	Cindy Blackburn
Jim Dean	Tim Barnes	Adrian Gonzalez	Jules Silverstein
		Lucy Steele	

12. Mar 7: Total food sales from the week are shown in the table below.

Item	Quantity Sold	Sales Price	Totals
Bottled Water	7	$1.50	$10.50
Sports Drink:			
Lemon		2.00	
Orange	4	2.00	8.00
Blue	2	2.00	4.00
Red	3	2.00	6.00
Energy Drink:			
Regular		3.75	
Sugar-Free	4	3.75	15.00
Nutrition Bar:			
Chocolate	5	3.25	16.25
Vanilla		3.25	
Peanut Butter	3	3.25	9.75
Subtotal			**69.50**
Sales Tax			**5.56**
Total			**75.06**

13. Mar 7: Deposited all Undeposited funds from the first week of the month into the checking account for a total of $1,050.06.

14. Mar 8: Richard Halpert paid $90 for a quarterly gym membership.

15. Mar 9: Check #1025 to Cody's Cleaning Co. in the amount of $250.00 for a complete gym cleaning (Janitorial Expense – Office/General Administrative type expense).

16. Mar 9: Pay Sales Taxes for sales taxes due through February 28 in the amount of $11.44.

    Note: Make sure to use the Record Tax Payment (Under Company > Sales Tax) and do not just write a check. Enter the correct payment date (03/09) and tax period date (02/28). 12

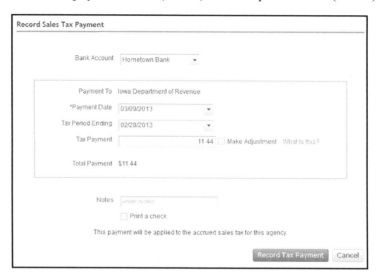

17. Mar 10: John Lockhart paid $25 for a first time gym registration fee and a monthly membership fee of $35.

18. Mar 10: Received payment of $35 from Robert Markum for March gym membership.

19. Mar 11: Paid bill from Cool T-shirts Co. with check #1026 in the amount of $45 (Make sure to change the date).

20. Mar 11: Purchase order #1002 to Fit Foods, Inc. in the amount of $91.86 to purchase the following inventory items (edit for the quantities ordered below):

Item	Quantity	Unit Cost	Total Cost	Sales Price
Bottled Water	48	$0.17	$8.16	$1.50
Sports Drink:				
Lemon	12	0.37	4.44	2.00
Orange	24	0.37	8.88	2.00
Blue	48	0.37	17.76	2.00
Red	6	0.37	2.22	2.00
Energy Drink:				
Regular	24	1.05	25.20	3.75
Sugar-Free	6	1.05	6.30	3.75
Nutrition Bar:				
Chocolate	24	0.45	10.80	3.25
Vanilla	12	0.45	5.40	3.25
Peanut Butter	6	0.45	2.70	3.25

21. Mar 11: Jack Sheppert paid $90 for a quarterly gym membership.

22. Mar 12: Received payment of $35 each from Daniel Brown and Adrian Gonzalez for March gym membership.

23. Mar 13: Kate Austino paid $25 for a first time gym registration fee and a monthly membership fee of $35.

24. Mar 14: Total food sales from the week are shown in the table below:

Item	Quantity Sold	Sales Price	Totals
Bottled Water	3	$1.50	$4.50
Sports Drink:			
Lemon	2	2.00	4.00
Orange		2.00	
Blue	1	2.00	2.00
Red	2	2.00	4.00
Energy Drink:			
Regular		3.75	
Sugar-Free	2	3.75	7.50
Nutrition Bar:			
Chocolate	1	3.25	3.25
Vanilla	1	3.25	3.25
Peanut Butter		3.25	
Subtotal			**28.50**
Sales Tax			**2.28**
Total			**30.78**

25. Mar 14: Deposited all Undeposited funds from the second week of the month into the checking account for a total of $435.78.

26. Mar 16: Received payment of $35 from Cindy Blackburn for March gym membership.

27. Mar 17: Sold 1 hour of personal training to Cindy Blackburn and Jim Dean for $35 each.

28. Mar 18: Jim Sawyer paid $25 for a first time gym registration fee and a monthly membership fee of $35.

29. Mar 19: Christian Sheppert paid $90 for a quarterly gym membership.

30. Mar 20: Sold 1 hour of personal training to Kate Austino for $35.

31. Mar 20: Received payment of $35 each from Jerry Kline and Tim Barnes for March gym membership.

32. Mar 21: Danielle Russell paid $25 for a first time gym registration fee and a monthly membership fee of $35.

33. Mar 21: Total food sales from the week are shown below:

Item	Quantity Sold	Sales Price	Totals
Bottled Water	5	$1.50	7.50
Sports Drink:			
Lemon		2.00	
Orange	2	2.00	4.00
Blue	3	2.00	6.00
Red	1	2.00	2.00
Energy Drink:			
Regular	3	3.75	
Sugar-Free		3.75	11.25
Nutrition Bar:			
Chocolate	3	3.25	9.75
Vanilla	1	3.25	3.25
Peanut Butter	2	3.25	6.50
Subtotal			**50.25**
Sales Tax			**4.02**
Total			**54.27**

34. Mar 21: Deposited all Undeposited funds from the third week of the month into the checking account for a total of $474.27.

35. Mar 22: Received partial inventory from purchase order #1002 from Fit Foods, Inc. Red sports drink was not available because it has been discontinued and Vanilla Energy Bars were out of stock.

Enter the bill for the receipt of all other items on the purchase for a total of $84.24. The terms are n/30.

Note: Enter a Bill and select Fit Foods which may recall the last bill for them. Click on 'Itemize by Product/Service' and if there are items and amounts already listed, click on 'Clear All Lines'. Then, click to 'Add Purchase Order' and edit the items to make Red Sports Drink and Vanilla Nutrition Bars both 0. The total should be $84.24.

36. Mar 24: Benny Linus paid $25 for a first time gym registration fee and a monthly membership fee of $35.

37. Mar 25: Issued a refund of $35 to Benny Linus who canceled his membership because he decided working out is too hard. (The refund was for the 1 month membership Benny purchased. The registration fee is non-refundable.) Write check #1027 for the refund.

38. Mar 26: Sent invoices to the following members in the amount of $35 for April membership (Monthly membership) with terms of n/30:

    - Adrian Gonzalez
    - Lucy Steele
    - Tim Barnes
    - Robert Markum
    - Katie Layton
    - John Lockhart
    - Kate Austino
    - Jim Sawyer

    Note: Jerry Kline, Daniel Brown, Cindy Blackburn, and Danielle Russell decided not to renew their membership.

39. Mar 27: Check #1028 to Rob's Repairs in the amount of $220.00 for repairing 2 broken machines.

40. Mar 28: Sold 2 hours of personal training to Adrian Gonzalez for $35.

41. Mar 30: Paid all bills for a total of $457.93 (assign check numbers 1029 to 1032 and enter correct payment date).

42. Mar 31: Received bill from Time Warner in the amount of $147.62 for phone, internet, and cable services with terms of n/30.

43. Mar 31: Received bill from Metro Electric Co. in the amount of $128.86 for electricity with terms of n/30.

44. Mar 31: Received bill from City of Springfield in the amount of for $79.45 for water with terms of n/30.

45. Mar 31: Received bill from Waste Management in the amount of $45.00 for trash removal with terms of n/30.

46. Mar 31: Total food sales from the week are shown in the table below:

Item	Quantity Sold	Sales Price	Totals
Bottled Water	10	$1.50	15.00
Sports Drink:			
Lemon	3	2.00	6.00
Orange	3	2.00	6.00
Blue	5	2.00	10.00
Red		2.00	
Energy Drink:			
Regular	5	3.75	18.75
Sugar-Free	2	3.75	7.50
Nutrition Bar:			
Chocolate	2	3.25	6.50
Vanilla	2	3.25	6.50
Peanut Butter	4	3.25	13.00
Subtotal			**89.25**
Sales Tax			**7.14**
Total			**96.39**

47. Mar 31: Deposited all Undeposited funds into the checking account for a total of $226.39.

Reconcile Accounts

Use the following information to reconcile the checking account:

Bank Statement Ending Date	3/31/2013
Bank Statement Ending Balance	$117,398.02
Outstanding Checks: Check # 1028 $220.00 Check # 1029 $147.62 Check # 1030 $178.86 Check # 1031 $86.45 Check # 1032 $45.00	Outstanding Deposits: 3/31/2013 $226.39

Checks and Payments

✓	Date	Type	Num	Payee	Amount
✓	02/28/2013	Bill Payment (Check)	1018	Time Warner	147.62
✓	02/28/2013	Bill Payment (Check)	1019	Metro Electric Co.	183.86
✓	02/28/2013	Bill Payment (Check)	1020	City of Springfield	51.45
✓	02/28/2013	Bill Payment (Check)	1021	Waste Management	45.00
✓	02/28/2013	Bill Payment (Check)	1022	Fit Foods, Inc.	126.48
✓	03/01/2013	Check	1023	Great American Bank	68.97
✓	03/06/2013	Check	1024	Copper Property Management Co.	1500.00
✓	03/08/2013	Check	1025	Cody's Cleaning Co.	250.00
✓	03/09/2013	Sales Tax Payment			11.44
✓	03/11/2013	Bill Payment (Check)	1026	Cool T-shirts Co.	45.00
✓	03/25/2013	Refund	1027	Benny Linus	35.00
	03/27/2013	Check	1028	Rob's Repairs	220.00
	03/30/2013	Bill Payment (Check)	1029	Time Warner	147.62
	03/30/2013	Bill Payment (Check)	1030	Metro Electric Co.	178.86
	03/30/2013	Bill Payment (Check)	1031	City of Springfield	86.45
	03/30/2013	Bill Payment (Check)	1032	Waste Management	45.00

Total checked(11) amount 2464.82

Use the following information to reconcile the Visa credit card account:

Bank Statement Ending Date	3/31/2013
Bank Statement Ending Balance	$56.70
Outstanding Items: None	

After reconciling the credit card account, select to write a check for payment now. Enter the payment date of Apr. 1, payable to Great American Bank with check number 1034.

Check Your Results

Create the following reports and compare them to the following reports. (Make sure to set the dates for March)

Balance Sheet

As of March 31, 2013

	Total
ASSETS	
Current Assets	
Bank Accounts	
Hometown Bank	116,862.24
Total Bank Accounts	**$116,862.24**
Accounts Receivable	
Accounts Receivable (A/R)	280.00
Total Accounts Receivable	**$ 280.00**
Other current assets	
Inventory Asset	132.36
Undeposited Funds	0.00
Total Other current assets	**$ 132.36**
Total Current Assets	**$117,274.60**
Fixed Assets	
Fitness Equipment	
Elliptical Machines	10,000.00
Free Weights	8,000.00
Stationary Bikes	12,000.00
Treadmills	10,000.00
Weight Machines	40,000.00
Total Fitness Equipment	**$ 80,000.00**
Leasehold Improvements	52,736.89
Office Furniture & Equipment	4,123.15
Outdoor Signage	1,200.00
Total Fixed Assets	**$138,060.04**
Other Assets	
Security Deposit	3,000.00
Total Other Assets	**$ 3,000.00**
TOTAL ASSETS	**$258,334.64**

LIABILITIES AND EQUITY

Liabilities		
Current Liabilities		
Accounts Payable		
Accounts Payable (A/P)		400.93
Total Accounts Payable	$	**400.93**
Credit Cards		
Visa		56.70
Total Credit Cards	$	**56.70**
Other Current Liabilities		
Iowa Department of Revenue Payable		19.00
Total Other Current Liabilities	$	**19.00**
Total Current Liabilities	$	**476.63**
Long-Term Liabilities		
Notes Payable - Hometown Bank		250,000.00
Total Long-Term Liabilities		**$250,000.00**
Total Liabilities		**$250,476.63**
Equity		
Joe Watson		
Joe Watson Partner Contribution		5,000.00
Total Joe Watson	$	**5,000.00**
Nancy Clemens		
Nancy Clemens Partner Contribution		5,000.00
Total Nancy Clemens	$	**5,000.00**
Opening Balance Equity		
Retained Earnings		
Tom Martin		
Tom Partner Contributions		5,000.00
Total Tom Martin	$	**5,000.00**
Net Income		-7,141.99
Total Equity	$	**7,858.01**
TOTAL LIABILITIES AND EQUITY		**$258,334.64**

Profit & Loss (Jan 01 - Mar 31)

January - March, 2013

	Jan 2013	Feb 2013	Mar 2013	Total
Income				
Gym Revenues		1,235.00	1,780.00	3,015.00
Registration Fees		175.00	150.00	325.00
Sales of Product Income		143.00	237.50	380.50
Total Income	$ 0.00	$ 1,553.00	$ 2,167.50	$ 3,720.50
Cost of Goods Sold				
Cost of Goods Sold		27.04	43.32	70.36
Inventory Shrinkage		6.30	1.70	8.00
Total Cost of Goods Sold	$ 0.00	$ 33.34	$ 45.02	$ 78.36
Gross Profit	$ 0.00	$ 1,519.66	$ 2,122.48	$ 3,642.14
Expenses				
Advertising	225.00	900.00		1,125.00
Cleaning Supplies		68.97		68.97
computer & Internet	550.00			550.00
Fitness Supplies		235.00		235.00
Janitorial			250.00	250.00
Legal & Professional Fees	1,785.00			1,785.00
Accounting Fees		450.00		450.00
Total Legal & Professional Fees	$ 1,785.00	$ 450.00	$ 0.00	$ 2,235.00
Office Expenses	136.67	56.70		193.37
Rent or Lease	1,500.00	1,500.00	1,500.00	4,500.00
Repair & Maintenance		75.00	220.00	295.00
Uniforms			45.00	45.00
Utilities				0.00
Electricity	183.86	178.86	128.86	491.58
Phone/Internet	147.62	147.62	147.62	442.86
Trash Removal	45.00	45.00	45.00	135.00
Water	51.45	86.45	79.45	217.35
Total Utilities	$ 427.93	$ 457.93	$ 400.93	$ 1,286.79
Total Expenses	$ 4,624.60	$ 3,743.60	$ 2,415.93	$ 10,784.13
Net Operating Income	-$ 4,624.60	-$ 2,223.94	-$ 293.45	-$ 7,141.99
Net Income	-$ 4,624.60	-$ 2,223.94	-$ 293.45	-$ 7,141.99

Accounts Receivable Aging Detail

As of March 31, 2013

	Date	Transaction Type	Num	Client	Due Date	Open Balance
Current						
	03/26/2013	Invoice	1070	Jim Sawyer	04/25/2013	35.00
	03/26/2013	Invoice	1069	Kate Austino	04/25/2013	35.00
	03/26/2013	Invoice	1068	John Lockhart	04/25/2013	35.00
	03/26/2013	Invoice	1063	Adrian Gonzalez	04/25/2013	35.00
	03/26/2013	Invoice	1066	Robert Markum	04/25/2013	35.00
	03/26/2013	Invoice	1065	Tim Barnes	04/25/2013	35.00
	03/26/2013	Invoice	1064	Lucy Steele	04/25/2013	35.00
	03/26/2013	Invoice	1067	Katie Layton	04/25/2013	35.00
Total for Current						**280.00**
TOTAL						**280.00**

Accounts Payable Aging Detail

As of March 31, 2013

	Date	Transaction Type	Vendor	Due Date	Past Due	Amount
Current						
	03/31/2013	Bill	Waste Management	04/30/2013	72	45.00
	03/31/2013	Bill	Time Warner	04/30/2013	72	147.62
	03/31/2013	Bill	Metro Electric Co.	04/30/2013	72	128.86
	03/31/2013	Bill	City of Springfield	04/30/2013	72	79.45
Total for Current						**400.93**
TOTAL						**400.93**

Sales by Customer Detail

March 2013

	Date	Transaction Type	Num	Product/Service	Qty	Rate	Amount
Adrian Gonzalez							
	03/07/2013	Sales Receipt	1044	Kardio Killers	1.00	50.00	50.00
	03/26/2013	Invoice	1063	Monthly Membership	1.00	35.00	35.00
	03/28/2013	Sales Receipt	1071	Personal Training	2.00	35.00	70.00
Total for Adrian Gonzalez							**155.00**
Allison Hoch							
	03/03/2013	Sales Receipt	1036	Quarterly	1.00	90.00	90.00
	03/07/2013	Sales Receipt	1039	Basic Fitness 101	1.00	50.00	50.00
Total for Allison Hoch							**140.00**
Benny Linus							
	03/24/2013	Sales Receipt	1061	Registration Fees	1.00	25.00	25.00
	03/24/2013	Sales Receipt	1061	Monthly Membership	1.00	35.00	35.00
	03/25/2013	Refund	1062	Monthly Membership	-1.00	35.00	-35.00
Total for Benny Linus							**25.00**
Christian Sheppert							
	03/19/2013	Sales Receipt	1057	Quarterly	1.00	90.00	90.00
Total for Christian Sheppert							**90.00**
Cindy Blackburn							
	03/07/2013	Sales Receipt	1046	Yoga Fitness	1.00	50.00	50.00
	03/17/2013	Sales Receipt	1054	Personal Training	1.00	35.00	35.00
Total for Cindy Blackburn							**85.00**
Danielle Russell							
	03/21/2013	Sales Receipt	1059	Monthly Membership	1.00	35.00	35.00
	03/21/2013	Sales Receipt	1059	Registration Fees	1.00	25.00	25.00
Total for Danielle Russell							**60.00**
Hugo Reyson							
	03/04/2013	Sales Receipt	1038	Quarterly	1.00	90.00	90.00
Total for Hugo Reyson							**90.00**
Jack Sheppert							
	03/11/2013	Sales Receipt	1051	Quarterly	1.00	90.00	90.00
Total for Jack Sheppert							**90.00**
Jerry Kline							
	03/07/2013	Sales Receipt	1043	Kardio Killers	1.00	50.00	50.00
Total for Jerry Kline							**50.00**
Jim Dean							
	03/03/2013	Sales Receipt	1035	Quarterly	1.00	90.00	90.00
	03/03/2013	Sales Receipt	1035	Personal Training	1.00	35.00	35.00
	03/07/2013	Sales Receipt	1040	Basic Fitness 101	1.00	50.00	50.00
	03/17/2013	Sales Receipt	1055	Personal Training	1.00	35.00	35.00
Total for Jim Dean							**210.00**
Jim Sawyer							
	03/18/2013	Sales Receipt	1056	Registration Fees	1.00	25.00	25.00
	03/18/2013	Sales Receipt	1056	Monthly Membership	1.00	35.00	35.00
	03/26/2013	Invoice	1070	Monthly Membership	1.00	35.00	35.00

Total for Jim Sawyer							**95.00**
John Brown							
	03/07/2013	Sales Receipt	1041	Wicked Weights	1.00	50.00	50.00
Total for John Brown							**50.00**
John Lockhart							
	03/10/2013	Sales Receipt	1050	Monthly Membership	1.00	35.00	35.00
	03/10/2013	Sales Receipt	1050	Registration Fees	1.00	25.00	25.00
	03/26/2013	Invoice	1068	Monthly Membership	1.00	35.00	35.00
Total for John Lockhart							**95.00**
Jules Silverstein							
	03/01/2013	Sales Receipt	1033	Quarterly	1.00	90.00	90.00
	03/07/2013	Sales Receipt	1047	Yoga Fitness	1.00	50.00	50.00
Total for Jules Silverstein							**140.00**
Kate Austino							
	03/13/2013	Sales Receipt	1052	Monthly Membership	1.00	35.00	35.00
	03/13/2013	Sales Receipt	1052	Registration Fees	1.00	25.00	25.00
	03/20/2013	Sales Receipt	1058	Personal Training	1.00	35.00	35.00
	03/26/2013	Invoice	1069	Monthly Membership	1.00	35.00	35.00
Total for Kate Austino							**130.00**
Katie Layton							
	03/03/2013	Sales Receipt	1037	Monthly Membership	1.00	35.00	35.00
	03/03/2013	Sales Receipt	1037	Registration Fees	1.00	25.00	25.00
	03/26/2013	Invoice	1067	Monthly Membership	1.00	35.00	35.00
Total for Katie Layton							**95.00**
Lucy Steele							
	03/07/2013	Sales Receipt	1045	Kardio Killers	1.00	50.00	50.00
	03/26/2013	Invoice	1064	Monthly Membership	1.00	35.00	35.00
Total for Lucy Steele							**85.00**
Lynn Sampson							
	03/01/2013	Sales Receipt	1034	Personal Training	1.00	35.00	35.00
Total for Lynn Sampson							**35.00**
Richard Halpert							
	03/08/2013	Sales Receipt	1049	Quarterly	1.00	90.00	90.00
Total for Richard Halpert							**90.00**
Robert Markum							
	03/26/2013	Invoice	1066	Monthly Membership	1.00	35.00	35.00
Total for Robert Markum							**35.00**
Tim Barnes							
	03/07/2013	Sales Receipt	1042	Wicked Weights	1.00	50.00	50.00
	03/26/2013	Invoice	1065	Monthly Membership	1.00	35.00	35.00
Total for Tim Barnes							**85.00**
Weekly Sales							
	03/07/2013	Sales Receipt	1048	Nutrition Bar:Chocolate	5.00	3.25	16.25
	03/07/2013	Sales Receipt	1048	Energy Drink:Sugar-Free	4.00	3.75	15.00
	03/07/2013	Sales Receipt	1048	Sports Drink:Blue Drink	2.00	0.37	0.74
	03/07/2013	Sales Receipt	1048	Sports Drink:Red Drink	3.00	0.37	1.11
	03/07/2013	Sales Receipt	1048	Bottled Water	7.00	0.17	1.19
	03/07/2013	Sales Receipt	1048	Nutrition Bar:Peanut Butter Bar	3.00	0.45	1.35
	03/07/2013	Sales Receipt	1048	Sports Drink:Orange Drink	4.00	0.37	1.48
	03/07/2013	Sales Receipt	1048	Nutrition Bar:Chocolate	5.00	0.45	2.25
	03/07/2013	Sales Receipt	1048	Energy Drink:Sugar-Free	4.00	1.05	4.20
	03/07/2013	Sales Receipt	1048	Energy Drink:Sugar-Free	-4.00	1.05	-4.20

Date	Type	Num	Item	Qty	Rate	Amount
03/07/2013	Sales Receipt	1048	Nutrition Bar:Chocolate	-5.00	0.45	-2.25
03/07/2013	Sales Receipt	1048	Sports Drink:Orange Drink	-4.00	0.37	-1.48
03/07/2013	Sales Receipt	1048	Nutrition Bar:Peanut Butter Bar	-3.00	0.45	-1.35
03/07/2013	Sales Receipt	1048	Bottled Water	-7.00	0.17	-1.19
03/07/2013	Sales Receipt	1048	Sports Drink:Red Drink	-3.00	0.37	-1.11
03/07/2013	Sales Receipt	1048	Sports Drink:Blue Drink	-2.00	0.37	-0.74
03/07/2013	Sales Receipt	1048	Sports Drink:Blue Drink	2.00	2.00	4.00
03/07/2013	Sales Receipt	1048	Sports Drink:Red Drink	3.00	2.00	6.00
03/07/2013	Sales Receipt	1048	Sports Drink:Orange Drink	4.00	2.00	8.00
03/07/2013	Sales Receipt	1048	Nutrition Bar:Peanut Butter Bar	3.00	3.25	9.75
03/07/2013	Sales Receipt	1048	Bottled Water	7.00	1.50	10.50
03/14/2013	Sales Receipt	1053	Sports Drink:Blue Drink	-1.00	0.37	-0.37
03/14/2013	Sales Receipt	1053	Sports Drink:Blue Drink	1.00	0.37	0.37
03/14/2013	Sales Receipt	1053	Bottled Water	3.00	0.17	0.51
03/14/2013	Sales Receipt	1053	Sports Drink:Red Drink	2.00	0.37	0.74
03/14/2013	Sales Receipt	1053	Sports Drink:Lemon	2.00	0.37	0.74
03/14/2013	Sales Receipt	1053	Energy Drink:Sugar-Free	2.00	1.05	2.10
03/14/2013	Sales Receipt	1053	Nutrition Bar:Vanilla Bar	1.00	0.45	0.45
03/14/2013	Sales Receipt	1053	Energy Drink:Sugar-Free	-2.00	1.05	-2.10
03/14/2013	Sales Receipt	1053	Sports Drink:Blue Drink	1.00	2.00	2.00
03/14/2013	Sales Receipt	1053	Nutrition Bar:Vanilla Bar	1.00	3.25	3.25
03/14/2013	Sales Receipt	1053	Nutrition Bar:Chocolate	1.00	3.25	3.25
03/14/2013	Sales Receipt	1053	Sports Drink:Red Drink	2.00	2.00	4.00
03/14/2013	Sales Receipt	1053	Sports Drink:Lemon	2.00	2.00	4.00
03/14/2013	Sales Receipt	1053	Bottled Water	3.00	1.50	4.50
03/14/2013	Sales Receipt	1053	Energy Drink:Sugar-Free	2.00	3.75	7.50
03/14/2013	Sales Receipt	1053	Sports Drink:Red Drink	-2.00	0.37	-0.74
03/14/2013	Sales Receipt	1053	Sports Drink:Lemon	-2.00	0.37	-0.74
03/14/2013	Sales Receipt	1053	Bottled Water	-3.00	0.17	-0.51
03/14/2013	Sales Receipt	1053	Nutrition Bar:Vanilla Bar	-1.00	0.45	-0.45
03/14/2013	Sales Receipt	1053	Nutrition Bar:Chocolate	-1.00	0.45	-0.45
03/14/2013	Sales Receipt	1053	Nutrition Bar:Chocolate	1.00	0.45	0.45
03/21/2013	Sales Receipt	1060	Nutrition Bar:Vanilla Bar	1.00	0.45	0.45
03/21/2013	Sales Receipt	1060	Sports Drink:Red Drink	1.00	0.37	0.37
03/21/2013	Sales Receipt	1060	Energy Drink:Regular	3.00	3.75	11.25
03/21/2013	Sales Receipt	1060	Nutrition Bar:Chocolate	3.00	3.25	9.75
03/21/2013	Sales Receipt	1060	Bottled Water	5.00	1.50	7.50
03/21/2013	Sales Receipt	1060	Nutrition Bar:Peanut Butter Bar	2.00	3.25	6.50
03/21/2013	Sales Receipt	1060	Sports Drink:Blue Drink	3.00	2.00	6.00
03/21/2013	Sales Receipt	1060	Sports Drink:Orange Drink	2.00	2.00	4.00
03/21/2013	Sales Receipt	1060	Nutrition Bar:Vanilla Bar	1.00	3.25	3.25
03/21/2013	Sales Receipt	1060	Sports Drink:Red Drink	1.00	2.00	2.00
03/21/2013	Sales Receipt	1060	Sports Drink:Red Drink	-1.00	0.37	-0.37
03/21/2013	Sales Receipt	1060	Nutrition Bar:Vanilla Bar	-1.00	0.45	-0.45
03/21/2013	Sales Receipt	1060	Sports Drink:Orange Drink	-2.00	0.37	-0.74
03/21/2013	Sales Receipt	1060	Bottled Water	-5.00	0.17	-0.85
03/21/2013	Sales Receipt	1060	Nutrition Bar:Peanut Butter Bar	-2.00	0.45	-0.90
03/21/2013	Sales Receipt	1060	Sports Drink:Blue Drink	-3.00	0.37	-1.11
03/21/2013	Sales Receipt	1060	Nutrition Bar:Chocolate	-3.00	0.45	-1.35
03/21/2013	Sales Receipt	1060	Energy Drink:Regular	-3.00	1.05	-3.15
03/21/2013	Sales Receipt	1060	Energy Drink:Regular	3.00	1.05	3.15

MICHELLE L. LONG AND ANDREW S. LONG

Date	Type	Num	Item	Qty	Rate	Amount
03/21/2013	Sales Receipt	1060	Nutrition Bar:Chocolate	3.00	0.45	1.35
03/21/2013	Sales Receipt	1060	Sports Drink:Blue Drink	3.00	0.37	1.11
03/21/2013	Sales Receipt	1060	Nutrition Bar:Peanut Butter Bar	2.00	0.45	0.90
03/21/2013	Sales Receipt	1060	Bottled Water	5.00	0.17	0.85
03/21/2013	Sales Receipt	1060	Sports Drink:Orange Drink	2.00	0.37	0.74
03/31/2013	Sales Receipt	1072	Energy Drink:Regular	5.00	3.75	18.75
03/31/2013	Sales Receipt	1072	Bottled Water	10.00	1.50	15.00
03/31/2013	Sales Receipt	1072	Nutrition Bar:Peanut Butter Bar	4.00	3.25	13.00
03/31/2013	Sales Receipt	1072	Sports Drink:Blue Drink	5.00	2.00	10.00
03/31/2013	Sales Receipt	1072	Energy Drink:Sugar-Free	2.00	3.75	7.50
03/31/2013	Sales Receipt	1072	Nutrition Bar:Chocolate	2.00	3.25	6.50
03/31/2013	Sales Receipt	1072	Nutrition Bar:Vanilla Bar	2.00	3.25	6.50
03/31/2013	Sales Receipt	1072	Sports Drink:Lemon	3.00	2.00	6.00
03/31/2013	Sales Receipt	1072	Sports Drink:Orange Drink	3.00	2.00	6.00
03/31/2013	Sales Receipt	1072	Nutrition Bar:Chocolate	-2.00	0.45	-0.90
03/31/2013	Sales Receipt	1072	Nutrition Bar:Vanilla Bar	-2.00	0.45	-0.90
03/31/2013	Sales Receipt	1072	Sports Drink:Lemon	-3.00	0.37	-1.11
03/31/2013	Sales Receipt	1072	Sports Drink:Orange Drink	-3.00	0.37	-1.11
03/31/2013	Sales Receipt	1072	Bottled Water	-10.00	0.17	-1.70
03/31/2013	Sales Receipt	1072	Nutrition Bar:Peanut Butter Bar	-4.00	0.45	-1.80
03/31/2013	Sales Receipt	1072	Sports Drink:Blue Drink	-5.00	0.37	-1.85
03/31/2013	Sales Receipt	1072	Energy Drink:Sugar-Free	-2.00	1.05	-2.10
03/31/2013	Sales Receipt	1072	Energy Drink:Regular	-5.00	1.05	-5.25
03/31/2013	Sales Receipt	1072	Energy Drink:Regular	5.00	1.05	5.25
03/31/2013	Sales Receipt	1072	Energy Drink:Sugar-Free	2.00	1.05	2.10
03/31/2013	Sales Receipt	1072	Sports Drink:Blue Drink	5.00	0.37	1.85
03/31/2013	Sales Receipt	1072	Nutrition Bar:Peanut Butter Bar	4.00	0.45	1.80
03/31/2013	Sales Receipt	1072	Bottled Water	10.00	0.17	1.70
03/31/2013	Sales Receipt	1072	Sports Drink:Lemon	3.00	0.37	1.11
03/31/2013	Sales Receipt	1072	Sports Drink:Orange Drink	3.00	0.37	1.11
03/31/2013	Sales Receipt	1072	Nutrition Bar:Chocolate	2.00	0.45	0.90
03/31/2013	Sales Receipt	1072	Nutrition Bar:Vanilla Bar	2.00	0.45	0.90

Total for Weekly Sales   **237.50**

TOTAL   **2,167.50**

Sales by Product/Service Detail

March 2013

	Date	Transaction Type	Num	Client	Qty	Rate	Amount
Basic Fitness 101							
	03/07/2013	Sales Receipt	1040	Jim Dean	1.00	50.00	50.00
	03/07/2013	Sales Receipt	1039	Allison Hoch	1.00	50.00	50.00
Total for Basic Fitness 101							**100.00**
Bottled Water							
	03/07/2013	Sales Receipt	1048	Weekly Sales	7.00	1.50	10.50
	03/07/2013	Sales Receipt	1048	Weekly Sales	-7.00	0.17	-1.19
	03/07/2013	Sales Receipt	1048	Weekly Sales	7.00	0.17	1.19
	03/14/2013	Sales Receipt	1053	Weekly Sales	3.00	0.17	0.51
	03/14/2013	Sales Receipt	1053	Weekly Sales	-3.00	0.17	-0.51
	03/14/2013	Sales Receipt	1053	Weekly Sales	3.00	1.50	4.50
	03/21/2013	Sales Receipt	1060	Weekly Sales	5.00	1.50	7.50
	03/21/2013	Sales Receipt	1060	Weekly Sales	-5.00	0.17	-0.85
	03/21/2013	Sales Receipt	1060	Weekly Sales	5.00	0.17	0.85
	03/31/2013	Sales Receipt	1072	Weekly Sales	10.00	0.17	1.70
	03/31/2013	Sales Receipt	1072	Weekly Sales	10.00	1.50	15.00
	03/31/2013	Sales Receipt	1072	Weekly Sales	-10.00	0.17	-1.70
Total for Bottled Water							**37.50**
Energy Drink							
Regular							
	03/21/2013	Sales Receipt	1060	Weekly Sales	3.00	1.05	3.15
	03/21/2013	Sales Receipt	1060	Weekly Sales	-3.00	1.05	-3.15
	03/21/2013	Sales Receipt	1060	Weekly Sales	3.00	3.75	11.25
	03/31/2013	Sales Receipt	1072	Weekly Sales	5.00	3.75	18.75
	03/31/2013	Sales Receipt	1072	Weekly Sales	5.00	1.05	5.25
	03/31/2013	Sales Receipt	1072	Weekly Sales	-5.00	1.05	-5.25
Total for Regular							**30.00**
Sugar-Free							
	03/07/2013	Sales Receipt	1048	Weekly Sales	4.00	1.05	4.20
	03/07/2013	Sales Receipt	1048	Weekly Sales	-4.00	1.05	-4.20
	03/07/2013	Sales Receipt	1048	Weekly Sales	4.00	3.75	15.00
	03/14/2013	Sales Receipt	1053	Weekly Sales	2.00	1.05	2.10
	03/14/2013	Sales Receipt	1053	Weekly Sales	2.00	3.75	7.50
	03/14/2013	Sales Receipt	1053	Weekly Sales	-2.00	1.05	-2.10
	03/31/2013	Sales Receipt	1072	Weekly Sales	2.00	1.05	2.10
	03/31/2013	Sales Receipt	1072	Weekly Sales	2.00	3.75	7.50
	03/31/2013	Sales Receipt	1072	Weekly Sales	-2.00	1.05	-2.10
Total for Sugar-Free							**30.00**
Total for Energy Drink							**60.00**
Kardio Killers							
	03/07/2013	Sales Receipt	1043	Jerry Kline	1.00	50.00	50.00
	03/07/2013	Sales Receipt	1045	Lucy Steele	1.00	50.00	50.00
	03/07/2013	Sales Receipt	1044	Adrian Gonzalez	1.00	50.00	50.00
Total for Kardio Killers							**150.00**
Monthly Membership							

	Date	Type	Num	Name	Qty	Rate	Amount
	03/03/2013	Sales Receipt	1037	Katie Layton	1.00	35.00	35.00
	03/10/2013	Sales Receipt	1050	John Lockhart	1.00	35.00	35.00
	03/13/2013	Sales Receipt	1052	Kate Austino	1.00	35.00	35.00
	03/18/2013	Sales Receipt	1056	Jim Sawyer	1.00	35.00	35.00
	03/21/2013	Sales Receipt	1059	Danielle Russell	1.00	35.00	35.00
	03/24/2013	Sales Receipt	1061	Benny Linus	1.00	35.00	35.00
	03/25/2013	Refund	1062	Benny Linus	-1.00	35.00	-35.00
	03/26/2013	Invoice	1065	Tim Barnes	1.00	35.00	35.00
	03/26/2013	Invoice	1064	Lucy Steele	1.00	35.00	35.00
	03/26/2013	Invoice	1063	Adrian Gonzalez	1.00	35.00	35.00
	03/26/2013	Invoice	1070	Jim Sawyer	1.00	35.00	35.00
	03/26/2013	Invoice	1069	Kate Austino	1.00	35.00	35.00
	03/26/2013	Invoice	1068	John Lockhart	1.00	35.00	35.00
	03/26/2013	Invoice	1066	Robert Markum	1.00	35.00	35.00
	03/26/2013	Invoice	1067	Katie Layton	1.00	35.00	35.00
Total for Monthly Membership							**455.00**
Nutrition Bar							
Chocolate							
	03/07/2013	Sales Receipt	1048	Weekly Sales	-5.00	0.45	-2.25
	03/07/2013	Sales Receipt	1048	Weekly Sales	5.00	0.45	2.25
	03/07/2013	Sales Receipt	1048	Weekly Sales	5.00	3.25	16.25
	03/14/2013	Sales Receipt	1053	Weekly Sales	1.00	3.25	3.25
	03/14/2013	Sales Receipt	1053	Weekly Sales	-1.00	0.45	-0.45
	03/14/2013	Sales Receipt	1053	Weekly Sales	1.00	0.45	0.45
	03/21/2013	Sales Receipt	1060	Weekly Sales	3.00	0.45	1.35
	03/21/2013	Sales Receipt	1060	Weekly Sales	-3.00	0.45	-1.35
	03/21/2013	Sales Receipt	1060	Weekly Sales	3.00	3.25	9.75
	03/31/2013	Sales Receipt	1072	Weekly Sales	-2.00	0.45	-0.90
	03/31/2013	Sales Receipt	1072	Weekly Sales	2.00	3.25	6.50
	03/31/2013	Sales Receipt	1072	Weekly Sales	2.00	0.45	0.90
Total for Chocolate							**35.75**
Peanut Butter Bar							
	03/07/2013	Sales Receipt	1048	Weekly Sales	-3.00	0.45	-1.35
	03/07/2013	Sales Receipt	1048	Weekly Sales	3.00	3.25	9.75
	03/07/2013	Sales Receipt	1048	Weekly Sales	3.00	0.45	1.35
	03/21/2013	Sales Receipt	1060	Weekly Sales	-2.00	0.45	-0.90
	03/21/2013	Sales Receipt	1060	Weekly Sales	2.00	0.45	0.90
	03/21/2013	Sales Receipt	1060	Weekly Sales	2.00	3.25	6.50
	03/31/2013	Sales Receipt	1072	Weekly Sales	4.00	0.45	1.80
	03/31/2013	Sales Receipt	1072	Weekly Sales	4.00	3.25	13.00
	03/31/2013	Sales Receipt	1072	Weekly Sales	-4.00	0.45	-1.80
Total for Peanut Butter Bar							**29.25**
Vanilla Bar							
	03/14/2013	Sales Receipt	1053	Weekly Sales	-1.00	0.45	-0.45
	03/14/2013	Sales Receipt	1053	Weekly Sales	1.00	3.25	3.25
	03/14/2013	Sales Receipt	1053	Weekly Sales	1.00	0.45	0.45
	03/21/2013	Sales Receipt	1060	Weekly Sales	1.00	3.25	3.25
	03/21/2013	Sales Receipt	1060	Weekly Sales	-1.00	0.45	-0.45
	03/21/2013	Sales Receipt	1060	Weekly Sales	1.00	0.45	0.45
	03/31/2013	Sales Receipt	1072	Weekly Sales	-2.00	0.45	-0.90
	03/31/2013	Sales Receipt	1072	Weekly Sales	2.00	3.25	6.50
	03/31/2013	Sales Receipt	1072	Weekly Sales	2.00	0.45	0.90

Total for Vanilla Bar							**13.00**
Total for Nutrition Bar							**78.00**
Personal Training							
	03/01/2013	Sales Receipt	1034	Lynn Sampson	1.00	35.00	35.00
	03/03/2013	Sales Receipt	1035	Jim Dean	1.00	35.00	35.00
	03/17/2013	Sales Receipt	1054	Cindy Blackburn	1.00	35.00	35.00
	03/17/2013	Sales Receipt	1055	Jim Dean	1.00	35.00	35.00
	03/20/2013	Sales Receipt	1058	Kate Austino	1.00	35.00	35.00
	03/28/2013	Sales Receipt	1071	Adrian Gonzalez	2.00	35.00	70.00
Total for Personal Training							**245.00**
Quarterly							
	03/01/2013	Sales Receipt	1033	Jules Silverstein	1.00	90.00	90.00
	03/03/2013	Sales Receipt	1035	Jim Dean	1.00	90.00	90.00
	03/03/2013	Sales Receipt	1036	Allison Hoch	1.00	90.00	90.00
	03/04/2013	Sales Receipt	1038	Hugo Reyson	1.00	90.00	90.00
	03/08/2013	Sales Receipt	1049	Richard Halpert	1.00	90.00	90.00
	03/11/2013	Sales Receipt	1051	Jack Sheppert	1.00	90.00	90.00
	03/19/2013	Sales Receipt	1057	Christian Sheppert	1.00	90.00	90.00
Total for Quarterly							**630.00**
Registration Fees							
	03/03/2013	Sales Receipt	1037	Katie Layton	1.00	25.00	25.00
	03/10/2013	Sales Receipt	1050	John Lockhart	1.00	25.00	25.00
	03/13/2013	Sales Receipt	1052	Kate Austino	1.00	25.00	25.00
	03/18/2013	Sales Receipt	1056	Jim Sawyer	1.00	25.00	25.00
	03/21/2013	Sales Receipt	1059	Danielle Russell	1.00	25.00	25.00
	03/24/2013	Sales Receipt	1061	Benny Linus	1.00	25.00	25.00
Total for Registration Fees							**150.00**
Sports Drink							
Blue Drink							
	03/07/2013	Sales Receipt	1048	Weekly Sales	-2.00	0.37	-0.74
	03/07/2013	Sales Receipt	1048	Weekly Sales	2.00	0.37	0.74
	03/07/2013	Sales Receipt	1048	Weekly Sales	2.00	2.00	4.00
	03/14/2013	Sales Receipt	1053	Weekly Sales	1.00	0.37	0.37
	03/14/2013	Sales Receipt	1053	Weekly Sales	-1.00	0.37	-0.37
	03/14/2013	Sales Receipt	1053	Weekly Sales	1.00	2.00	2.00
	03/21/2013	Sales Receipt	1060	Weekly Sales	-3.00	0.37	-1.11
	03/21/2013	Sales Receipt	1060	Weekly Sales	3.00	2.00	6.00
	03/21/2013	Sales Receipt	1060	Weekly Sales	3.00	0.37	1.11
	03/31/2013	Sales Receipt	1072	Weekly Sales	-5.00	0.37	-1.85
	03/31/2013	Sales Receipt	1072	Weekly Sales	5.00	0.37	1.85
	03/31/2013	Sales Receipt	1072	Weekly Sales	5.00	2.00	10.00
Total for Blue Drink							**22.00**
Lemon							
	03/14/2013	Sales Receipt	1053	Weekly Sales	2.00	0.37	0.74
	03/14/2013	Sales Receipt	1053	Weekly Sales	-2.00	0.37	-0.74
	03/14/2013	Sales Receipt	1053	Weekly Sales	2.00	2.00	4.00
	03/31/2013	Sales Receipt	1072	Weekly Sales	3.00	2.00	6.00
	03/31/2013	Sales Receipt	1072	Weekly Sales	3.00	0.37	1.11
	03/31/2013	Sales Receipt	1072	Weekly Sales	-3.00	0.37	-1.11
Total for Lemon							**10.00**

Orange Drink

03/07/2013	Sales Receipt	1048	Weekly Sales	-4.00	0.37	-1.48
03/07/2013	Sales Receipt	1048	Weekly Sales	4.00	2.00	8.00
03/07/2013	Sales Receipt	1048	Weekly Sales	4.00	0.37	1.48
03/21/2013	Sales Receipt	1060	Weekly Sales	2.00	0.37	0.74
03/21/2013	Sales Receipt	1060	Weekly Sales	-2.00	0.37	-0.74
03/21/2013	Sales Receipt	1060	Weekly Sales	2.00	2.00	4.00
03/31/2013	Sales Receipt	1072	Weekly Sales	-3.00	0.37	-1.11
03/31/2013	Sales Receipt	1072	Weekly Sales	3.00	0.37	1.11
03/31/2013	Sales Receipt	1072	Weekly Sales	3.00	2.00	6.00

Total for Orange Drink — **18.00**

Red Drink

03/07/2013	Sales Receipt	1048	Weekly Sales	3.00	2.00	6.00
03/07/2013	Sales Receipt	1048	Weekly Sales	-3.00	0.37	-1.11
03/07/2013	Sales Receipt	1048	Weekly Sales	3.00	0.37	1.11
03/14/2013	Sales Receipt	1053	Weekly Sales	2.00	0.37	0.74
03/14/2013	Sales Receipt	1053	Weekly Sales	2.00	2.00	4.00
03/14/2013	Sales Receipt	1053	Weekly Sales	-2.00	0.37	-0.74
03/21/2013	Sales Receipt	1060	Weekly Sales	-1.00	0.37	-0.37
03/21/2013	Sales Receipt	1060	Weekly Sales	1.00	2.00	2.00
03/21/2013	Sales Receipt	1060	Weekly Sales	1.00	0.37	0.37

Total for Red Drink — **12.00**

Total for Sports Drink — **62.00**

Wicked Weights

03/07/2013	Sales Receipt	1042	Tim Barnes	1.00	50.00	50.00
03/07/2013	Sales Receipt	1041	John Brown	1.00	50.00	50.00

Total for Wicked Weights — **100.00**

Yoga Fitness

03/07/2013	Sales Receipt	1047	Jules Silverstein	1.00	50.00	50.00
03/07/2013	Sales Receipt	1046	Cindy Blackburn	1.00	50.00	50.00

Total for Yoga Fitness — **100.00**

TOTAL — **2,167.50**

Inventory Valuation Summary

As of March 31, 2013

	Total		Avg Cost
	Qty	Asset Value	
Bottled Water	53.00	9.01	0.17
Energy Drink			
Regular	40.00	42.00	1.05
Sugar-Free	6.00	6.30	1.05
Total Energy Drink		$ 48.30	
Nutrition Bar			
Chocolate	30.00	13.50	0.45
Peanut Butter Bar	19.00	8.55	0.45
Vanilla Bar	15.00	6.75	0.45
Total Nutrition Bar		$ 28.80	
Sports Drink			
Blue Drink	50.00	18.50	0.37
Lemon	24.00	8.88	0.37
Orange Drink	34.00	12.58	0.37
Red Drink	17.00	6.29	0.37
Total Sports Drink		$ 46.25	
TOTAL		$ 132.36	

Transaction List by Date

Date	Transaction Type	Num	Name	Account	Split	Amount
03/01/2013	Check	1023	Great American Bank	Hometown Bank	Visa	-68.97
03/01/2013	Sales Receipt	1033	Jules Silverstein	Undeposited Funds	Gym Revenues	90.00
03/01/2013	Sales Receipt	1034	Lynn Sampson	Undeposited Funds	Gym Revenues	35.00
03/02/2013	Bill		Cool T-shirts Co.	Accounts Payable (A/P)	Uniforms	45.00
03/03/2013	Sales Receipt	1035	Jim Dean	Undeposited Funds	-Split-	125.00
03/03/2013	Sales Receipt	1036	Allison Hoch	Undeposited Funds	Gym Revenues	90.00
03/03/2013	Sales Receipt	1037	Katie Layton	Undeposited Funds	-Split-	60.00
03/04/2013	Payment		Lucy Steele	Undeposited Funds	Accounts Receivable (A/R)	35.00
03/04/2013	Inventory Qty Adjust	2		Inventory Shrinkage	Inventory Asset	
03/04/2013	Sales Receipt	1038	Hugo Reyson	Undeposited Funds	Gym Revenues	90.00
03/06/2013	Check	1024	Copper Property Management Co.	Hometown Bank	Rent or Lease	-1,500.00
03/07/2013	Sales Receipt	1039	Allison Hoch	Undeposited Funds	Gym Revenues	50.00
03/07/2013	Sales Receipt	1040	Jim Dean	Undeposited Funds	Gym Revenues	50.00
03/07/2013	Sales Receipt	1041	John Brown	Undeposited Funds	Gym Revenues	50.00
03/07/2013	Sales Receipt	1042	Tim Barnes	Undeposited Funds	Gym Revenues	50.00
03/07/2013	Sales Receipt	1043	Jerry Kline	Undeposited Funds	Gym Revenues	50.00
03/07/2013	Sales Receipt	1044	Adrian Gonzalez	Undeposited Funds	Gym Revenues	50.00
03/07/2013	Sales Receipt	1045	Lucy Steele	Undeposited Funds	Gym Revenues	50.00
03/07/2013	Sales Receipt	1046	Cindy Blackburn	Undeposited Funds	Gym Revenues	50.00
03/07/2013	Sales Receipt	1047	Jules Silverstein	Undeposited Funds	Gym Revenues	50.00
03/07/2013	Sales Receipt	1048	Weekly Sales	Undeposited Funds	-Split-	75.06
03/07/2013	Deposit			Hometown Bank	-Split-	1,050.06
03/08/2013	Sales Receipt	1049	Richard Halpert	Undeposited Funds	Gym Revenues	90.00
03/09/2013	Check	1025	Cody's Cleaning Co.	Hometown Bank	Janitorial	-250.00
03/09/2013	Sales Tax Payment			Hometown Bank	-Split-	11.44
03/10/2013	Sales Receipt	1050	John Lockhart	Undeposited Funds	-Split-	60.00
03/10/2013	Payment		Robert Markum	Undeposited Funds	Accounts Receivable (A/R)	35.00
03/11/2013	Bill Payment (Check)	1026	Cool T-shirts Co.	Hometown Bank	Accounts Payable (A/P)	-45.00
03/11/2013	Purchase Order	1003	Fit Foods, Inc.	Accounts Payable (A/P)	-Split-	91.86
03/11/2013	Sales Receipt	1051	Jack Sheppert	Undeposited Funds	Gym Revenues	90.00
03/12/2013	Payment		Daniel Brown	Undeposited Funds	Accounts Receivable (A/R)	35.00
03/12/2013	Payment		Adrian Gonzalez	Undeposited Funds	Accounts Receivable (A/R)	35.00
03/13/2013	Sales Receipt	1052	Kate Austino	Undeposited Funds	-Split-	60.00
03/14/2013	Sales Receipt	1053	Weekly Sales	Undeposited Funds	-Split-	30.78
03/14/2013	Deposit			Hometown Bank	-Split-	435.78
03/16/2013	Payment		Cindy Blackburn	Undeposited Funds	Accounts Receivable (A/R)	35.00
03/17/2013	Sales Receipt	1054	Cindy Blackburn	Undeposited Funds	Gym Revenues	35.00
03/17/2013	Sales Receipt	1055	Jim Dean	Undeposited Funds	Gym Revenues	35.00
03/18/2013	Sales Receipt	1056	Jim Sawyer	Undeposited Funds	-Split-	60.00
03/19/2013	Sales Receipt	1057	Christian Sheppert	Undeposited Funds	Gym Revenues	90.00
03/20/2013	Sales Receipt	1058	Kate Austino	Undeposited Funds	Gym Revenues	35.00
03/20/2013	Payment		Jerry Kline	Undeposited Funds	Accounts Receivable (A/R)	35.00
03/20/2013	Payment		Tim Barnes	Undeposited Funds	Accounts Receivable	35.00

QUICKBOOKS ONLINE PRACTICE SET

Date	Type	Num	Name	Account	Split	Amount
03/21/2013	Sales Receipt	1059	Danielle Russell	Undeposited Funds	-Split-	60.00
03/21/2013	Sales Receipt	1060	Weekly Sales	Undeposited Funds	-Split-	54.27
03/21/2013	Deposit			Hometown Bank	-Split-	474.27
03/21/2013	Bill		Fit Foods, Inc.	Accounts Payable (A/P)	-Split-	84.24
03/24/2013	Sales Receipt	1061	Benny Linus	Undeposited Funds	-Split-	60.00
03/25/2013	Refund	1062	Benny Linus	Hometown Bank	Gym Revenues	-35.00
03/26/2013	Invoice	1063	Adrian Gonzalez	Accounts Receivable (A/R)	Gym Revenues	35.00
03/26/2013	Invoice	1064	Lucy Steele	Accounts Receivable (A/R)	Gym Revenues	35.00
03/26/2013	Invoice	1065	Tim Barnes	Accounts Receivable (A/R)	Gym Revenues	35.00
03/26/2013	Invoice	1066	Robert Markum	Accounts Receivable (A/R)	Gym Revenues	35.00
03/26/2013	Invoice	1067	Katie Layton	Accounts Receivable (A/R)	Gym Revenues	35.00
03/26/2013	Invoice	1068	John Lockhart	Accounts Receivable (A/R)	Gym Revenues	35.00
03/26/2013	Invoice	1069	Kate Austino	Accounts Receivable (A/R)	Gym Revenues	35.00
03/26/2013	Invoice	1070	Jim Sawyer	Accounts Receivable (A/R)	Gym Revenues	35.00
03/27/2013	Check	1028	Rob's Repairs	Hometown Bank	Repair & Maintenance	-220.00
03/28/2013	Sales Receipt	1071	Adrian Gonzalez	Undeposited Funds	Gym Revenues	70.00
03/30/2013	Bill Payment (Check)	1029	Time Warner	Hometown Bank	Accounts Payable (A/P)	-147.62
03/30/2013	Bill Payment (Check)	1030	Metro Electric Co.	Hometown Bank	Accounts Payable (A/P)	-178.86
03/30/2013	Bill Payment (Check)	1031	City of Springfield	Hometown Bank	Accounts Payable (A/P)	-86.45
03/30/2013	Bill Payment (Check)	1032	Waste Management	Hometown Bank	Accounts Payable (A/P)	-45.00
03/30/2013	Bill Payment (Check)	1033	Fit Foods, Inc.	Hometown Bank	Accounts Payable (A/P)	-84.24
03/31/2013	Bill		Time Warner	Accounts Payable (A/P)	Utilities:Phone/Internet	147.62
03/31/2013	Bill		Metro Electric Co.	Accounts Payable (A/P)	Utilities:Electricity	128.86
03/31/2013	Bill		City of Springfield	Accounts Payable (A/P)	Utilities:Water	79.45
03/31/2013	Bill		Waste Management	Accounts Payable (A/P)	Utilities:Trash Removal	45.00
03/31/2013	Sales Receipt	1072	Weekly Sales	Undeposited Funds	-Split-	96.39
03/31/2013	Deposit			Hometown Bank	-Split-	226.39

Made in the USA
Lexington, KY
30 April 2014